I0558931

Advance Praise for *At Ease*

"*At Ease* is the insightful and pragmatic wealth of information that I wish I'd had as a military veteran new to the business world. Save yourself a lot of confusion by putting to work this must-have blueprint for any military veteran who cares not just about career success as a civilian, but happiness as well."

　　　—Peter Jensen, PhD, Lieutenant Colonel, US Army (Retired)

"Emily King is the expert on how both veterans and employers can successfully navigate the transition from a military to a private-sector career. In *At Ease*, she generously shares her two decades of experience in coaching leaders on both sides of that transition to provide a practical and actionable road map for mutual success and satisfaction."

　　　—Scott Eblin, globally recognized executive coach and best-selling
author of *The Next Level: What Insiders Know About Executive Success*

"*At Ease* is a road map to an empowered transition from military service to civilian employment. Make no mistake: it is a major life change, but it doesn't have to be a grind. Author Emily King is an accomplished thought leader and expert in this arena. This book should be in the hands of every veteran seeking to make a successful transition."

　　　—Jon Sanchez, former US Navy SEAL
CEO Team Performance Institute

"*At Ease: The Guide to a Smooth and Successful Military Transition* stands apart from other books about career transitions by the author's insights into what makes military transitions unique and the effectiveness of the approach outlined in the book. Because it looks beyond the externalities of job descriptions and résumés into internal factors such as purpose, values, and personal leadership and culture, this book is an especially valuable resource for family members and professional coaches supporting the transitioning military person."

—Frank Ball
Faculty Member, Georgetown University Leadership Coaching Program (2000–2014) and Marine for life

"Every service member looking at transition needs to read *At Ease* for the real story on what you'll experience, and tools for dealing with it. As the author says, military transition is about so much more than a résumé. It is about purpose and mission, and this book is an invaluable tool for that objective."

—Greg Gadson, Colonel, US Army (Retired)
Actor, speaker, and author of *Finding Waypoints: A Warrior's Journey Toward Peace and Purpose*

AT EASE

The Guide to a Smooth and Successful Military Transition

Emily King

Copyright © 2024 Emily King

ALL RIGHTS RESERVED
No part of this book may be translated, used, or reproduced in any form or by any means, in whole or in part, electronic or mechanical, including photocopying, recording, taping, or by any information storage or retrieval system without express written permission from the author or the publisher, except for the use in brief quotations within critical articles and reviews.

info@grandinetta.com

Limits of Liability and Disclaimer of Warranty:
The authors and/or publisher shall not be liable for your misuse of this material. The contents are strictly for informational and educational purposes only.

Warning—Disclaimer:
The purpose of this book is to educate and entertain. The authors and/or publisher do not guarantee that anyone following these techniques, suggestions, tips, ideas, or strategies will become successful. The author and/or publisher shall have neither liability nor responsibility to anyone with respect to any loss or damage caused, or alleged to be caused, directly or indirectly by the information contained in this book. Further, readers should be aware that Internet websites listed in this work may have changed or disappeared between when this work was written and when it is read.

Edited by: Frank Steele
Cover and interior design by Stefan Merour

Published by Fullcourt Press
Printed and bound in the United States of America

ISBN:
Paperback: 979-8-9914657-0-0
Ebook: 979-8-9914657-1-7

Library of Congress Control Number: 2024919296

Publisher's Cataloging-in-Publication Data

Names: King, Emily, 1965-, author.

Title: At ease / Emily King.

Description: Philadelphia, PA: Fullcourt Press, 2024.

Identifiers: LCCN: 2024919296 | ISBN: 979-8-9914657-0-0 (paperback) | 979-8-9914657-1-7 (ebook)

Subjects: LCSH Retired military personnel--United States--Handbooks, manuals, etc. | Retired military personnel--Employment--United States. | Veterans--Employment--United States. | Veterans--Services for--United States. | Career changes--United States. | Vocational guidance--United States. | BISAC BUSINESS & ECONOMICS / Careers / Career Advancement & Professional Development | HISTORY / Military / United States | SELF-HELP / Personal Growth / General
Classification: LCC UB357 .K56 2024 | DDC 355.115--dc23

Dedicated to veterans, reservists,
and active-duty service members of
the United States Armed Forces,
and the organizations
that hire them.

Contents

Foreword

By Col. Brad Wenstrup, DPM, US Army Reserve (Ret.), member of Congress

I met Emily King through a mutual friend who described her as someone dedicated to the welfare of our nation's military service members and veterans. She is passionate about eliminating the divide that still exists between military and civilian cultures and has dedicated considerable energy, time, and talent to helping people on both sides who are moving through this complex and sometimes fraught journey. As an early thought leader on this topic, Emily's expertise has been sought by Army generals and corporate CEOs alike. Her first book, *Field Tested,* is a seminal guide for both veterans and business leaders since its release in 2011, helping countless veterans and their employers to avoid or mitigate predictable pitfalls. Now, more than a decade later, Emily again steps into uncharted territory by lifting the veil on what remains undiscussed: the emotional and psychological impact of military transition. As a retired U.S. Army Reserve Colonel, veteran of the Iraq War, and lawmaker dedicated to veterans issues, I am honored to be part of this important book.

My own career as physician, military officer and, in more recent years, member of Congress, has offered multiple perspectives on the realities of military service and how we can best serve those who served our country. I was deeply moved by a story Emily shared with me the first time we met. In response to a question I asked about her dedication to veterans issues, even though she herself has never served, she told me about a poignant moment that inspired her life's mission. Her client, a recently retired colonel, had been assessed by his civilian superiors as lacking basic leadership skills. He was distraught, and incredulous; Emily was at a loss and wanted answers. As a behavioral scientist, Emily launched an organization-wide study of other leaders. Her results were shocking. Most, if not all, former military leaders struggled to succeed there, and for similar reasons. Emily's solution included targeted coaching and training, which resulted in an about-face for her client and the company at large. At Johns Hopkins University, she expanded her study to other large employers of military officers and replicated her findings. The problem was not a lack of leadership, but a lack of translation from one strong culture to another: the complex cultural difference between leading in the military and leading in the private sector. That was twenty years ago.

Today, this subject continues to be lost in the noise of "how to write a resume," and "how to find a job." Those are important tasks, but they do not constitute military transition, which is, fundamentally, not about executing tasks, but about strategic analysis of Self. Without this, a veteran may find a job (or two, or three) before facing the hard reality that they have lost their sense of purpose, mission, and identity. This is often a moment of crisis for veterans—and this book can help lead them on the journey of discovery that should really begin in the earliest days of transition from military service. We need to do better at preparing veterans for this task.

Military service isn't just a career, and the transition from service to civilian employment requires more than just help with resumes and job hunting; it requires focus on individual well-being during the transition from service to civilian life. Imagine how much better our military recruitment could be if we embraced this approach from day one and strove to prepare veterans for the best first civilian job imaginable. We could exponentially improve the available talent pool if we did so. Our military, our veterans, and the civilian organizations that hire them, would all benefit if we stopped presenting military service as a self-identity with a lifetime commitment, and instead as an important step in the career ladder of a successful professional.

A lofty yet worthy aspiration. In the meantime, hundreds of thousands of extremely capable military service members separate each year, and unfortunately too many do not have the information and tools available to successfully navigate the significant life change that is military transition. In my experience, as a Reservist, I was fortunate and accustomed to both the civilian and military workforce leadership roles—not all service members have that opportunity. *At Ease* is a book that hands veterans (and their employers!) the tools needed so they can bring their significant experience and leadership not just to the next job, but to the next chapter of success in their lives.

Introduction

At Ease is radically different from other books on the topic of military transition, most of which focus on the tactics of résumé writing and job search. This is not my definition of military transition. As a behavioral scientist, organizational consultant, and Master Certified Coach, my perspective is strategic, looking at root causes and solving for them in sustainable ways. Both perspectives are needed; finding a job is important. The greater challenge for service members, I've found, is finding a new purpose and mission. Individuals and organizations succeed faster when the human aspects of military transition have been properly cared for.

Unlike my first book, *Field Tested,* which was written primarily for employers, *At Ease* is written primarily for (1) current and former military service members embarking on the transition to civilian employment, and (2) military veterans whose transition has been rocky and who seek a more effective approach that gets better results or who seek a new approach to finding satisfaction in post-military employment. I believe smart organizations will read *At Ease* for the insight it offers about the military talent segment and make it available to new hires, their managers, and Human Resource teams. While *Field Tested* has been widely read and acclaimed by service members and employers alike, the challenges it foretold persist all these years later. Hence, *At Ease*.

As a result of actively engaging with *At Ease*, service members and veterans will be poised to find far more than just a job, but to find themselves and who they want to be without the uniform. That will go a long way toward finding *the right job*, not just any job. Hiring organizations using *At Ease* will be better positioned to achieve favorable business outcomes and return on investments made in military talent.

Context

Twenty years ago when my work and research began on this subject, the concept of military transition was new. It began with a consulting assignment with a large defense contracting firm, where retired military officers were struggling to succeed in leadership roles. My job was to figure out why, and fix it. One officer interview was especially memorable. He was a newly retired Army colonel who had just received an unsatisfactory rating on his first civilian performance review. The cause? "Lack of effective leadership." Understandably, he was baffled, distraught, and hungry for assistance. Together we learned and mastered this thing I dubbed "military transition."

This dynamic echoed across the organization, revealing highly thematic root causes I was able to solve for. I was both intrigued and deeply concerned by the profound impact it had on people who had served the nation for decades. It seemed inconceivable that a proven leader in one field could so quickly lose value in another. This experience led me to conduct original research at Johns Hopkins University on the subject of challenges faced by senior military officers transitioning to civilian business leadership roles, and the impact of those challenges on business outcomes.

A passion was awakened in me to help current and former military service members and civilian employers succeed with one another, to alleviate what I came to see as widespread and unnecessary suffering associated with military transition. Findings of my research are referenced in *Field Tested*.

About *At Ease*

- **Emphasis on the psychology of transition**, the human experience of it, and the challenges faced in the process. I aim to be of service by making sense of it and giving it meaning. By doing so, my goal is to empower employers with insight and tools that produce positive business outcomes.

- **Amplification of the coach's perspective,** to shed light on the habits of thought and behavior that can impede a smooth military transition, and practical tips for high-impact mindsets and approaches for civilian success. Based on two decades of experience coaching service members, veterans, and civilian line managers, this feature alone differentiates *At Ease* from other books on the subject of military transition. We pride ourselves on a solid track record of success in easing the transition for military new hires and their employers, and accelerating cultural integration.

- **A new Chapter 1**, focused on the truth of military transition: it is much more than a résumé and interview skills; it is about the personal transformation needed for success.

- **Updates to all chapters**, based on our collective learning over the last twelve years, about how to accelerate learning and achieve self-awareness and actionable insight.
- **Removal of tactical topics** pertaining to résumés, interviews, and job search. In the years following *Field Tested,* the market was flooded with books on these topics, covering them in greater detail than I could. Topics related to the employee lifecycle (recruitment to separation) are addressed here at a high level, in terms of key insights, learning, and best practices that have evolved since the publication of *Field Tested.*
- **Increased the interactive component** by doubling the number of activities designed to help readers apply what they're learning as they go through the book. Permission—in fact, encouragement—to write in the margins, and in ink if you'd like!
- **Introduced new resources** developed since *Field Tested.* Specifically, the "Accelerated Military Transition Course," created to reach as many transitioning service members and hiring organizations as possible (https://military.grandinetta.com).

Throughout the book you will see quotes from former service members who share their personal experiences with the transition from military service to civilian employment. I personally interviewed and surveyed each of these individuals, who represent most branches of military service and both enlisted and officer ranks. All quotes are from former service members, used with their permission.

Another feature carried over from *Field Tested* is what I call "Coaching Conversations," which illustrate real-world challenges through dialogue. They demonstrate the value of coaching to accelerate learning during the transition process. These are inspired by but not taken from actual situations.

Learning Objectives

For transitioning service members and veterans: To maximize your learning, **approach this book with an open mind. Civilian practices may seem unfamiliar or even strange at first. Remember, different doesn't always mean wrong. Suspend judgment and embrace curiosity to uncover the value that's here for you.** I offer a new perspective for your consideration.

The primary learning objectives you can expect to achieve by engaging with *At Ease* are to increase your professional success in nonmilitary organizations by:

- Confronting the most challenging aspects of military transition
- Identifying and explaining key cultural differences
- Raising your awareness of transition pitfalls and how to avoid them
- Sharing lessons learned from a host of veterans who achieved success
- Providing real-world examples and activities to help you grow

For organizations and employers: This book's primary objectives are to increase your success with employees who are/were military service members by accelerating cultural integration and time-to-performance, and increasing retention.

Primary learning objectives you can expect to achieve by engaging with *At Ease* are to increase your level of insight and awareness regarding the valuable talent segment comprised of current and former service members, and get the most out of your genuine desire for mutual success by:

- Applying the insights and tools in your everyday job
- Anticipating and heading off challenges related to the military-to-civilian transition
- Using proven tools like the "Cultural Translator" to add value right away with new hires
- Optimizing new-hire engagement by mastering Days 1–90

For all readers: As I've said, the primary audience for *At Ease* is the current and former military service member, and the secondary audience is the private sector/civilian employer. **It may be tempting to skip over portions that don't seem to apply to you, such as Chapter 1 (aimed at service members) and Chapter 2 (aimed at employers). I encourage you to avoid this temptation. An essential benefit for all readers is insight to the mindset and assumptions common to each group (service member and employer).** Everyone's raised awareness will contribute to smooth and successful military transition.

Part 1

Situational Awareness

About this section:

What: Foundational perspectives for current and former service members and civilian employers

Who: Written for the benefit of all readers

Why: To provide an orientation to the topic of military transition

How: Through research, anecdotes, theoretical models, and application exercises

Chapter 1

Veterans: There's More Than What They Told You

"When you get out, it's kind of like a shock to the system. … It took a long time to find my place, my niche. It was very tough after being in a job where you're the top guy and you know what you're doing and people seek you out as the expert, for your opinions."

—ENLISTED SERVICE MEMBER, USAF[1]

Understanding the Landscape: What Are the Top Transition Challenges?

MILITARY TRANSITION IS NOT ABOUT A RÉSUMÉ. Let me repeat: *MILITARY TRANSITION IS NOT ABOUT A RÉSUMÉ.*

Military transition is fundamentally about personal transformation.

Military transition is a term I coined two decades ago to describe the struggle to succeed in the civilian workplace after military service.

It was never about résumés or interviews but, rather, the deeply human and personal experience of a major life change. It is about identity, culture, personal growth, humility, and resilience. In this way, military transition is similar to many life changes any one of us might face; however, the transition veterans make from military to civilian employment involves a unique set of challenges.

The résumé is a tactical tool for getting a job. Very different topic. Your actual transition from the military will happen, whether you have a good résumé or not. **A quality transition means letting go of the old, swimming in the unknown and, if you follow a good framework like the Military Transition Framework™ provided here, you will gradually find yourself working as naturally in a civilian job as you did in the military.** Those who focus on their résumé and interview skills <u>instead</u> of the transition process will likely go through several unhappy civilian jobs before realizing they are the common denominator in the unhappiness. A better way forward is to use your terminal leave as an opportunity to address the transition or, if you have to jump into a civilian job right away to keep the paychecks coming, address the transition as an after-hours priority. However you do it, *At Ease* will be your guide to a smooth and successful military transition.

To further define the nature of military transition, it is helpful to put a structure around it—a way of understanding what's happening, why it's happening, and when to declare victory over it. Later in *At Ease*, I will share a framework I developed which has helped countless veterans make sense and meaning of the transition. But first, let's get on the same page regarding the anatomy of a life transition as big as this one will be (or has been) for you.

The Root of the Issue: Why These Challenges Occur

Many years ago, William Bridges wrote a book called *Transitions: Making Sense of Life's Changes*.[2] I highly recommend you read this book. In it, Bridges observes that transitions in life tend to happen in three stages. Success is defined as experiencing each stage fully, along with its emotions, lessons, losses, and gains. I have used the Bridges model with coaching clients for years, both veterans and civilians alike, and the model of military transition presented herein is surely inspired by Bridges's classic book. Here's a high-level overview of Bridges's three stages of transition:

1. *Endings.* Using the metaphor of a boat on the water, the ending is what lies behind you—the shore you are leaving. It's crucial to acknowledge and process your feelings about what you're leaving behind. Trying to skip this stage can leave you emotionally anchored to the past, making it difficult to move forward.

Your feelings are valid. It's important to let yourself experience the mix so you can move forward on your journey. When we hang on to the shore—anchor ourselves to it—we can't easily move on. It is important to press on.

2. *Neutral Zone.* This phase of transition is when you are in the middle of the water, with no sight of either shore. You are literally "out there." It's often the most challenging part of the journey due to its ambiguity. Remember, this phase is temporary, but it's essential for growth and preparation. Embrace it as an opportunity for learning and self-discovery.

3. *New Beginnings.* At last, you see the shore! This last stage feels more comfortable, but it requires careful consideration. How do you want to approach this new landing place? Success in this phase means arriving without unnecessary baggage from the past, with a clear sense of who you are and how you want to contribute, ready to embrace new opportunities and ways of operating.

Navigating the Journey: How to Address Each Challenge

What to Focus On

Understand, I am not telling you to blow off your résumé. All the tactical things you are doing to secure employment are important to keeping a paycheck coming in. *But they have nothing to do with mastering the life transition you are in.* You want to be focusing now on who you are without the military. That is what this transition is really all about. You can work the tactics alongside this if you want to; in fact, they will be enhanced by the insights gained in *At Ease*.

Mastering Transition

The biggest mistake I've seen veterans make over and over: expecting military transition to be "just another change of duty station." It is not. It is a significant life event that you want to be ready for. Interestingly, the most common question I get from employers is "What's the biggest pitfall we should avoid when hiring veterans?" My answer will sound familiar: underestimating the significance of the cultural transition. The good news for employers and veterans alike is that the pitfalls are highly thematic, meaning I have seen the same ones for decades across countless individuals and organizations, and have proven practices for avoiding them. I offer them here for your consideration.

The two critical skills for mastering the military transition are *reflection* and *informed action.* Why reflection? Because it leads to **self-awareness**. Why informed action? Because it enables you to **respond** to your new environment from a place of **choice** rather than gut reaction. Throughout *At Ease*, you will find usable insight about these skills, starting right now.

Deepening Self-Awareness and Taking Informed Action

The activities in this book are designed to boost your self-awareness, a critical component of a successful military transition. This heightened self-knowledge enables you to take purposeful, informed action rather than uninformed action, otherwise known as reaction.

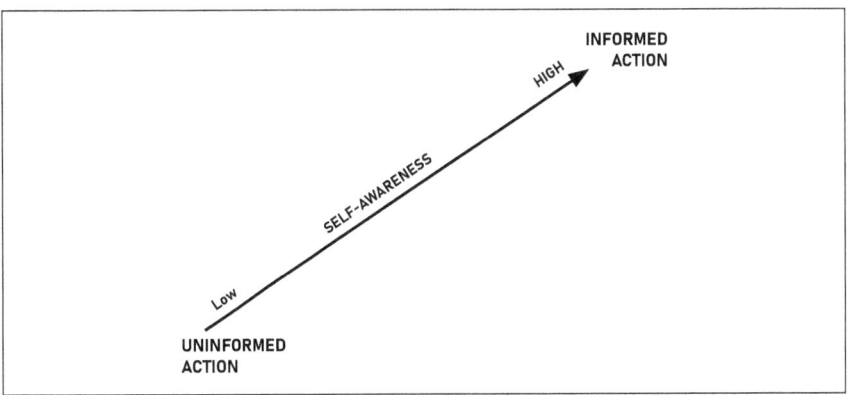

The goal is to progress from reactive, uninformed decisions to decisions and actions grounded in self-awareness and insight. Why? So the actions you take lead to the outcomes you desire. Reflection leads to self-awareness and insights. Putting those insights into action means meaningful, purposeful action. Informed action.

Self-awareness is the result of looking inward and learning about oneself. It is often the painful moments in life that yield the greatest amount of self-awareness, like receiving difficult feedback or experiencing a setback in an area we have worked hard to master, or unfamiliar situations that put us outside our comfort zone. In coaching leaders and teams, I celebrate the "aha moment" when something comes together in a new way that is usable and valuable. Building self-awareness can be hard, painful, liberating, exciting; most importantly, it is the threshold to having more choice and control in our lives.

How does self-awareness work?

Without self-awareness, we're just out there in the world operating however we operate and hoping for a good outcome. Sometimes that works. Sometimes, however, life or the people in it throw us a curveball and we experience a jolt of surprise by the impact of just being ourselves. If you've ever asked yourself, "Did I really just say/do that?" you are on the edge of an aha moment. If you double-click on your question and reflect further, you may gain valuable self-awareness and a new choice in your life. Continue your inquiry: "Okay, that is not what I meant to say/do … why did it happen?" The answer is, likely, a new level of self-awareness. Continue: "That did not go over well and I don't want to say/do it again … how can I ensure I don't repeat this mistake?" The answer to this last question equates to a new choice, whereas before, you simply reacted instinctively. Now, based on your new awarenesses (I did or said something I didn't mean to, it got a poor reaction, I have an idea of why it happened, and I think I know how to prevent it in the future), you can get to work on new habits that produce better outcomes. And, in the process, feel more in charge of yourself rather than subject to your automatic reactions to life.

As we gain self-awareness, we find that we are less likely to be caught off guard by our own thoughts, feelings, actions, and outcomes. We can now predict what might challenge us, how we want to handle those situations or people, and take informed action rather than being overtaken by gut reaction. We can work with ourselves—coach ourselves—through unpredictable events because we are no longer unpredictable to ourselves.

Your military service has surely provided opportunities to build self-awareness, and some people will make more use of them than others. Regardless, leaving the military and entering the civilian workforce will be a reset. Some of what you know about yourself will apply to this new context, and some of it won't. Military transition is largely about the process of figuring out what you know and have that will work, and learning what won't and how to quickly replace it with new information about yourself and the world. This is a complex, confusing, and disorienting process for many veterans. I wrote this book and its predecessor *Field Tested* to help you get through it as smoothly as possible.

Coping with Loss of Identity

My research with Johns Hopkins University found that, while veterans with 10+ years of service faced numerous practical challenges, the most pervasive issue across all levels and tenures of military service was a profound loss of identity. The intensity of this identity loss correlated with length of service, but even those with shorter terms reported experiencing it to some degree.

The loss of one's identity is a deeply distressing experience. "Scary," "disorienting," "lonely," and "lost" are feelings often reported by recently and not-so-recently separated service members. This sense of loss is understandable given that military service encompasses not just a job, but an entire way of life and community. Your kids go to school with your coworkers' kids, play sports together, celebrate the key milestones of growing up together. The all-encompassing nature of military identity is often only fully realized once it's gone, during the transition to civilian life.

To begin exploring this for yourself, let's jump into an activity called "Taking Off the Uniform." The name refers to something I still hear to this day from employers of veterans. When they want to hire my firm to provide executive coaching for veterans, they say something to the effect of, "He's still in uniform." That is shorthand for "hasn't made the military transition yet," and we know just how to help. As you work through the following activity, remember that it's normal to feel a range of emotions. Transition is a process. The insights you gain from this exercise will serve as a foundation as you continue to work through the activities in this book and navigate your journey to civilian life.

Practical Application:

Activity—Taking Off the Uniform

After years or decades in uniform, removing it can be traumatic. Why? Because it has been part of your identity—it tells yourself and others about your position in the organization and your accomplishments. To thrive outside the military, the first order of operations is to figure out who you are without the uniform. The longer you've served, the tougher the adjustment.

Purpose: Explore what the uniform has meant to you and how you do/will feel about hanging it up for good.

Directions: Reflect on the following questions before responding as candidly as possible. If you have not yet separated from service, try to imagine how it will feel to operate 24/7 out of uniform.

1. My uniform communicates/communicated the following about me:

_____

_____

2. In uniform I feel/felt:

_____

_____

3. In uniform, I expect(ed) this from others:

_____

_____

4. The thought of life without a uniform leaves me feeling:

_____

_____

5. Without the uniform, I am defined by:

_____

_____

6. Without the uniform, I have the opportunity to:

_____

_____

Allow yourself to reflect on your responses, as more insight may come to the surface as you continue through this chapter.

Why is identity such a big deal? Because a robust sense of identity provides us with stable footing; it tells us who we are. Without it, we will often feel lost and alone. In times of uncertainty, we do the only thing we know: what we've done before. However, in the context of military transition, these old patterns often prove ineffective. In his insightful book *Deep Change*, author Robert Quinn states, "A map we have used in the past might be of limited value in new territory. In a new situation, if we cling to our old map, we might become deeply frustrated." Quinn goes on to say, "We continue to explore our new and problematic territory with an old map, and that makes our problems worse. Our certainty that our old map must work drives us into a state of great pain. ... Only when our pain gets excruciating are we willing to humble ourselves and consider new actions that might allow us to successfully progress in our new situation."[3]

So how does one navigate this challenging terrain? Quinn references Joseph Campbell's concept of "the hero's journey," which is a story of epic transition—truly a transformation of one's identity. Quinn says, "In embarking on the journey, we must leave the world of certainty. We must courageously journey to a strange place where there are a lot of risks and much is at stake, a place where there are new problems that require us to think in new ways."[4]

Moving Forward: Action Steps for Success

Learning to Think in New Ways

The field of leadership development has embraced a concept called "growth mindset," which is also sweeping the corporate world as the cornerstone of many executive training programs. It has been long established by professional coaches as a key principle for developing leaders. I reference it here as a highly effective and relevant tool for your military transition.

Growth mindset emerged from the research of Stanford University psychologist Carol Dweck, who specializes in the psychology of motivation and mindset. Simply put, it posits that there are two ways of operating in the world: with a "fixed" mindset or a "growth" mindset. While individuals can exhibit different mindsets depending on the context, fostering an overall growth mindset will be helpful to navigating your transition successfully.

Dweck has described fixed-mindset individuals as dreading failure because it is a negative statement about basic abilities that make up their identity and self-esteem. A person with a fixed mindset believes their self-worth as a person is based on how well they can perform in a certain area, with failure seen as something to avoid because it feels bad on a deep level.

On the other hand, a person with a growth mindset doesn't fear failure as much because they have perspective about their performance. Specifically, they know that their performance does not define them—it is not tied to their sense of identity; furthermore, performance can be improved; and finally, they value the learning that comes from failure.

According to Dweck, these two mindsets play an important role in all aspects of a person's life; she argues that the growth mindset allows a person to live a less stressful and more successful life. [5]

To help you apply Dweck's theory to your own life and military transition, I offer the following distinctions, which you are encouraged to experiment with and reword to be of most value:

Fixed Mindset	Topic	Growth Mindset
This is not how we did it in the military; this is wrong (and I am right).	Operations	This is different, not necessarily wrong. There is a lot I don't yet know about how to succeed in this new context.
I achieved rank in the military, and that should matter to civilian employers and colleagues.	Role	My military rank doesn't have context here; with time I will establish myself in the civilian workplace.
Mission comes first, always, whatever it takes.	Mission	Mission is important but different in the civilian workplace. I need to listen, observe, and ask about priorities.
Communication should be succinct and efficient because we depend on it to execute work.	Communication	Communication is a way of building relationships; every communication is an opportunity to build or break trust.
Trust is absolute; colleagues should have my back like I'd have theirs.	Trust	Absolute trust isn't needed in all relationships. I'm curious about how this works in civilian life.

How do you see fixed and growth mindsets at work in yourself? It's helpful to explore this. Funny example: After decades of using the concept with clients and in my own life, I recently had an aha moment of my own related to something I've felt stuck about for years. I realized that the reason I could not keep my desk organized was that I have never kept it organized over time. I realized several things about this: first, it is untrue that I have never had an organized desk; second, I have organized it many times successfully; third, my issue is maintaining organization, not achieving it; my inner narrative about being a fundamentally messy person has prevented me from overcoming the pattern; oh my gosh, I have a fixed mindset about it! No wonder I've been stuck. As soon as I realized all of this, I felt completely empowered to integrate a few new habits that will lead me to sustained success—and I proceeded to do so. As a result, I no longer identify as a messy person due to the condition of my desk.

Look for evidence of your own fixed mindset as you proceed through this book and your military transition. Why? Because maintaining a fixed mindset only makes the road harder. Let's not do that to ourselves.

In her groundbreaking book *Mindset: Changing the Way You Think to Fulfill Your Potential*, Dweck poses a question worth your consideration: "What are the consequences of thinking that your intelligence or personality is something you can develop, as opposed to something that is a fixed, deep-seated trait?"[6]

Reflection Exercise: Contemplate and journal about this question, considering its implications for your transition journey.

_____

_____

_____

_____

_____

_____

_____

_____

_____

_____

_____

_____

_____

_____

_____

_____

_____

_____

_____

_____

Now that you've begun to explore the important topics of mindset, identity, and self-awareness, you can expect them to be ever-present in your day-to-day life. Continue to take notes and reflect on these concepts as you navigate your transition.

Closing Thoughts

We have covered a lot of ground in this chapter, and I hope you see military transition in a new light, as so much more than résumés and job interviews. It is about you and your life. For employers, it is a glimpse into what veteran new hires may be experiencing and, I hope, will spark ideas for how you can support them in their successful transition. Regardless of your role, *At Ease* is filled with ideas, best practices, and real-world advice from veterans who have faced and overcome the challenge of military transition. My intention is to be your coach through the process, so you can feel confident that you are in good hands and know that you are not alone. So many have gone before you and, through *At Ease* and *Field Tested,* want to help you avoid the pitfalls they experienced in their military transition.

Chapter 2

Employers: Prepare for Success

"There needs to be some guidance on how to work in the civilian world, especially for people who went into the military after high school and it's all they know. ... they think that's how the world operates."

—ENLISTED SERVICE MEMBER, USAF[7]

Understanding the Landscape: What Are the Key Considerations for Employers?

THIS CHAPTER PROVIDES AN OVERVIEW OF CHARACTERISTICS SHARED AMONG MANY VETERANS, how they manifest in the civilian workplace, and common misperceptions. Veterans as a group are not monolithic; to the contrary, they are diverse in all the ways other groups are diverse. We've learned a lot about intersectionality since *Field Tested* was released in 2011, and have much learning left to do on the subject.

Employers are much smarter today than they were twelve-plus years ago, having experienced the employment lifecycle of veterans many times over, as they have with other talent segments. Progress has been made at the organizational level to even the playing field for veteran new hires; for example, use of established sourcing channels, veteran-focused messages and value propositions and, in many large organizations, vibrant employee resource groups. I know because I designed many of them.

In spite of programmatic steps forward, we at Grandinetta Group continue to see requests for very basic content related to military transition, and to hear the same types of concerns from veteran new hires that we did fifteen years ago. For example, many tell us that new-hire orientation offers little value in terms of describing culture, norms, performance standards, success criteria, career opportunities, or reward systems. Despite the government's transition training, the military-civilian divide persists in terms of cultural understanding and actual readiness for success in the civilian workplace.

Engaging with *At Ease* presents you with a good opportunity to take a fresh look at your programs and culture through the lens of veterans. Small moves get small gains; bold moves can meaningfully impact your business. Is your organization fully realizing return on its investment in the form of accelerated time-to-performance, business outcomes, and retention?

I challenge and encourage you to approach this topic with new eyes and a spirit of creativity. My hope is that you will find new ideas and energy for optimizing the veteran experience and increasing business impact.

The Root of the Issue: Why Hire Veterans?

Characteristic Strengths

Let's start with a very basic question: Why hire a veteran? Set aside all of the other considerations like altruism and patriotism and look at what they as a group bring in terms of competence and productivity. There are some key characteristics of military service that benefit civilian organizations, such as early training and accountability for leadership. Even a young person with only a few years of service will bring skills and experience rarely found in their civilian peers. Veterans with any length of service have worked in teams to accomplish tangible outcomes with limited resources of time and materials. The potential upside of employing veterans is clear. Following are just a few of the shared assets we see in the veteran talent segment:

- Loyalty
- Mission Driven
- Discipline
- Ownership/Accountability
- Leadership
- Strategy
- Bringing Order to Chaos
- Important Credentials

Some of these may look obvious, but keep reading and you'll be surprised at how they reveal themselves and positively impact a civilian work environment. Your opportunity as employers is to provide an environment in which these obvious assets can shine.

Loyalty

I often hear loyalty cited by employers as a key characteristic of military talent. It can be, but veterans, like any civilian new hires, have the potential to be long-term employees **if they have reason to stay**. A manager's genuine concern for the welfare of their employees is highly correlated with high employee engagement and retention. In the military, a high level of involvement is ingrained in the leadership philosophy. For example, in the military, your immediate superior knows you, probably knows your family, and is concerned about you as a member of the community on and off the job. It is that manager's job to "take care of" the team, which can mean being brought into team members' personal lives, celebrations, and challenges of all types. The sense of community contributes to loyalty and may be instructive to civilian managers striving for loyal employees and high retention.

Note for transitioning service members: you will see and feel this difference when you become a civilian employee. Outside of the military, your personal privacy comes first, and managers are actually prohibited from getting too personal by a variety of laws. Know that going in, so it doesn't come across as a harsh surprise—and so it doesn't feel personal, as if they don't care about you. You will see throughout this book how harmful assumptions can be and how easily they are made.

Mission Driven

The military, across branches of service, has a very strong culture, as anybody who observes it from the outside can tell. The military has specific ways of doing things, procedure and protocol, which are necessary to serve its mission. Most civilian organizations don't ask employees to be on call 24/7, but the military does. It's the way to serve the mission. Commitment to the mission is not a platitude but a cornerstone of military culture, baked into everyday operating procedures. It is cultivated from Day One in each individual member, who then brings that felt experience to your civilian organization. Does your civilian organization have a clearly articulated mission understood by all? Do the standards and expectations for behavior map back to that mission so they are mutually reinforcing? If so, you may be a great fit for veterans. If not, you may be leaving the asset of being mission driven on the table.

Discipline

This characteristic is often associated with the military, but what does it mean? Does it mean getting up at the crack of dawn, hitting the gym, and cleaning the house before leaving for work in the morning? In the military, discipline means doing things the right way even if the right way takes longer to accomplish; it means following protocol to the letter to ensure consistent results, rather than increasing risk by improvising. Discipline is viewed as an operating principle, a way of being, the "right" way to get things done. Discipline is a character strength in the military that in the civilian world translates to employees you can count on to see a task through to completion and to do so under extremely stressful conditions.

In the words of a former enlisted service member, "The military attitude is 'adapt and overcome.' There's nothing we can't do—it might take longer, but we'll do it."[8]

Ownership/Accountability

In the military, you are issued the tools required to do your job. It is your responsibility to maintain and account for those tools, and frequent inventory inspections ensure that no one is caught without the tools they need. If a junior enlisted service member loses his wrench and then has to report it lost as part of the inspection process, the cost of the wrench comes out of his paycheck, unless he can replace it himself before reporting it. In either case, he is paying to replace the lost government-issued wrench. That's all there is to it. By ensuring that the individual has a personal stake in the proper procedures and protection of assets, each individual quickly learns to take time and care to protect those assets. The individual who loses his wrench once will undoubtedly take full ownership of the replacement so as to protect the asset. Ownership and accountability are characteristic of the military way of operating, and service members bring this to the civilian workplace. They expect to be given responsibility, be held accountable for results, and be rewarded with additional responsibility. Does your organization have a culture and method of promoting from within? Is good performance expected and recognized? If so, it may be a great fit for a veteran. If not, chances are all employees, not just veterans, would respond favorably to improvement in these areas.

Leadership

Any length of military service—even just one three-year tour of duty—will include training and experience in leadership. Leadership begins in Basic Training and continues throughout the career of a service member. When you stop to think about it, the one thing that makes the military run effectively is a constant pipeline of leaders at every level (rank) in the hierarchy. Nobody invests in leadership training like the U.S. military.

One outcome of this leadership culture is a consistent point of view from veterans that you won't get from the average civilian. In the civilian workplace, people can advance into management roles based on business results (e.g., sales figures) rather than on demonstrated leadership skills and ability. There can be a world of difference between words on a résumé and real-time, on-the-ground effectiveness. On the other hand, when it comes to military service members, you can be sure that they do have some degree of administrative management ability, if not higher-level leadership strength. Does your organization invest in hiring, developing, and retaining high-caliber leaders at all levels?

Does it have high standards for effective leadership of people as well as of tasks, and for accountability and rewarding excellence in others? If so, veterans may thrive in your organization. If not, they and other employees may find it challenging to work with poor leaders.

Strategy

The size of the military and the scope of its mission mean that personnel, especially those with responsibility for squads or units, are exposed to large-scale operations. *Everything* is a large-scale operation when you think about it. For example, moving five hundred people across the globe by sea for an eighteen-month deployment is a complicated process to plan and execute, but not uncommon in the military. For this reason, veterans can often conceive of strategy and change at a larger scale than the average civilian who hasn't led a complex operation with lots of moving parts. This is not to say that everyone comes out of the service with strategy experience, but they *have* been part of a huge machine, a huge organization, and they have been part of making it work. How will your organization make the best and highest use of this asset?

Bringing Order to Chaos

This is in some ways a summary of all previous strengths. Military service members often have experience working with lots of moving parts that need to be organized. This includes structuring processes and coordinating large groups of people. This allows them to envision order where someone else might be overwhelmed. For example, consider a team that doesn't communicate or get along and that misses deadlines and has a reputation for being difficult to work with. To the average manager, this can look like one big nightmare to deal with. A veteran, on the other hand, might look at it and immediately see a path to order and getting things on track. A veteran may not know how to tactically accomplish it in a civilian organization, but he or she will likely be able to visualize an outcome based on the diverse experiences that were part of military service. How can you position veteran new hires to demonstrate this value to the business?

Important Credentials

The military heavily invests time and money toward training service members. Consequently, many have received extensive (and expensive!) technical training and certifications. This represents a tremendous cost savings to civilian organizations that hire veterans. Likewise, many recent service members have pre-existing security clearances, which are of great value to government employers, defense agencies, and civilian organizations.

Navigating the Journey: How to Address Challenges and Leverage Strengths

Applying What You've Learned

A great way of increasing engagement and business impact of veterans is to facilitate a dialogue about the assets described in this chapter. If your organization has an employee resource group (ERG) for veterans/military, they might jump at the chance to organize a community dialogue about how they experience the organization. The dialogue could include topics such as:

1. How was each asset demonstrated in the military? How do you see it valued here?
2. To what extent are you able to showcase these assets in our organization?
3. What barriers have you encountered?
4. What opportunities do you see for us as an organization?
5. How could our existing programs be improved for veterans? (e.g., new hire orientation, career development opportunities, mentoring)

For the best outcome, ensure it's a two-way dialogue, not a one-way focus group. The value is in the mutual learning that occurs by sharing insights and experiences, and in creating solutions together.

By completing this exercise, you'll be better prepared to integrate veterans into your workforce and create an environment where they can thrive and contribute their unique assets and experiences.

Practical Application:

Organizational Readiness Assessment

Now that we've reviewed some of the assets military veterans can bring to the table, let's see if the table will be able to hold them. The following article was published years ago by ASTD (now ATD, the Association for Talent Development) and still holds true today. It is a structured way of refreshing your view of an organization's readiness to succeed with the veterans it hires.

- -

Organizational Readiness Assessment

In preparing to hire military veterans, you need to first determine if your organization is ready to meet the challenge and take full advantage of these skilled employees. Assemble a cross-functional stakeholder group and engage in honest self-reflection as an organization. The following are high-level categories of questions to consider, along with an example of each. Your answers to the following questions can be the basis of a business case in support of veteran programs.

1. Rationale and Requirements

How serious and/or urgent is this request? Is there commitment among decision-makers?

2. Organizational Context

What's happening in the organization now? Where are time and resources being focused?

3. Organizational Insight

What is our previous experience with veterans?

4. Recruitment

Have we ever attempted to recruit from the military? If so, what can we learn from experience?

5. Engagement and Retention

What retention data (quantitative or anecdotal) do we have about those veterans we have hired in the past?

6. Performance Management

How have former military service members performed in our organization?

7. Career Management

Have veterans progressed within our organization? If so, what factors contributed to their success?

8. Goals and Outcomes

What do we want our end-state to look like? How will things be different and how will that help the business?

9. Measurement and Evaluation

How will we know change has occurred? What reference points (performance ratings, retention data, employee engagement surveys) will we use as a baseline to measure our progress?

Source: Emily King, "Military to Civilian Onboarding," ASTD *InfoLine*, Vol. 27, Issue 1013, 2010. Used with permission from the American Society of Training and Development.

I suggest you respond to each question yourself based on instinct, and a second time with the help of a cross-functional team made up of someone from Human Resources, Recruitment, Training, DEI, Benefits, and Organization Development. Engaging all People functions will yield a robust view of the current state and enroll key stakeholders. The exercise has often led to tangible results, in the form of data-based business cases for investment in veteran programs.

Closing Thoughts

Civilian organizations and veterans have so much to offer one another! I encourage you as an employer to refresh your commitment and goals pertaining to veteran employees. With a little creativity, you can positively impact business outcomes and employee satisfaction among this valued talent segment. Are you getting the most out of your military/veteran ERG? How can you strengthen that partnership to fully engage them in ways that are meaningful for all? The possibilities are without limit, and I can't wait to hear about all the new best practices you develop along the way.

The bottom line is that when you hire a veteran, you stand to bring somebody into your organization who (1) is accustomed to having to get things done, (2) is resourceful, doing it with little thought to their own self-interest, and (3) keeps the mission and the organization in mind. This is a strong place to start, regardless of the cultural learning curve that may follow. After all, think about all the time and money that organizations spend in an effort to instill those qualities in their employees. There are incentive programs, motivational giveaways and prizes, team-building events that attempt to engender a sense of commitment to the organization and to the work itself—all with various degrees of effectiveness. In contrast, the military cultivates an extraordinary degree of employee engagement without such extras, and the service members you hire bring that high level of engagement with them. Your challenge is to earn and sustain engagement by having a veteran-friendly culture. This brings us to our next topic: cultural differences between military and civilian organizations and how to bridge the gap.

Chapter 3

It's All About Culture

"The biggest lesson I've had to learn as a results-driven person is that, in the civilian world, how you accomplish something is just as important as the merit of the accomplishment itself."

—OFFICER, USMC[9]

Understanding the Landscape: What Are the Key Cultural Differences?

IT'S NO SURPRISE THAT MILITARY SERVICE MEMBERS come to the civilian workforce with a unique mindset. As a result, the transition from one organizational culture to the other is often fraught with missteps or, to put a positive spin on it, "on-the-job training." A manifestation of this transition challenge is that military service members may not ask for help or seek resources because they aren't aware of their own need. Absent information or feedback to the contrary, they may see their methods as being effective when they are not. This creates an imperative for line managers and internal HR professionals to be prepared to provide proactive support. A smooth and successful transition contributes directly to success and retention, as evidenced by the most common reasons given for leaving a civilian job: lack of fit and difficulty adapting to new ways of doing things.

What is **organizational culture**? We can think of it as the personality of an organization, the characteristics we would use to describe what it's like to work there. Every organization has its own culture, and some are stronger than others. The military has a very strong culture, which we'll explore in a moment. Civilian organizations can be very different from one another, but likely share some characteristics.

Culture is made up of the spoken and unspoken rules of conduct unique to an organization. For example, speaking and behaving in a manner that respects others and doesn't discriminate is often a written policy of large organizations. Small organizations may not have a documented policy but an unstated "understanding" that discriminatory behavior is unacceptable. Just about everyone, veteran or civilian, has had a misstep or two due to this being an unstated "understanding." Hopefully, it leads to self-awareness!

Unspoken/assumed expectations can occur in most organizations regardless of size. Once in a while you may encounter something that is a stated value or rule, but it is not evident in day-to-day operation. For example, a stated value may be "Respect"; however, in day-to-day work life, one may see examples of employees regarding each other with a lack of respect. This can be challenging, and I've found it's helpful to guard against cynicism in such moments and allow things to play out so we can learn from them.

Try to be open so you can learn as much as possible by listening, observing, asking questions, and seeking feedback. *At Ease* is readiness training for veterans and employers alike. Keep reading!

The Challenge of Culture Change

Employers: Imagine leaving your retirement party after twenty years with a civilian company. You have a lot to show for those twenty years and a lot to be proud of. You also have another ten years to work if you so wish. You decide to join the military as a senior leader with deep functional expertise in the field of learning and development. You look forward to the challenge of implementing your proven best practices in a new organization.

It is your first day. Your new boss greets you. Do you know what to call her? Jane? Mrs. Smith? Ma'am? With her is your new assistant. What do you call him? Private? Joe? Deputy? Kiddo, because he looks so young?

After a while, you are asked to prepare a simple memo regarding a routine training policy. Do you know how to write so people will understand it and take action? Do you use a casual, friendly tone? Collegial? Or formal—perhaps using a standard format of some kind?

As the lunch hour approaches, you are feeling good about the work you've accomplished on the policy memo and you are looking forward to sending it off to your boss. You attach it to an email, which you close with "Best," and your name. Fortunately she knows you're on a learning curve, so she isn't too irritated when she comes into your office with a hard copy of the email and the comment, "This is not appropriately written. You need to close with 'V/r,' meaning Very Respectfully, then your name. Oh, and if the person you're emailing is a peer, it is just 'r/.' And if you are emailing subordinates, drop the 'r/.'"

What a downer. You've gotten your first bit of corrective feedback before your policy memo even got reviewed. You have many very basic questions and it isn't even noon. This job change is going to be much harder and take far longer than you or anyone else had expected. Already you may have inadvertently demoted your boss and insulted your assistant just by the way you addressed them. Never mind the nuances of working in this particular division; it feels as though you have been dropped into another world entirely.

This scenario is unlikely to happen in real life. For one thing, the military does not generally hire professionals from industry in mid-career. Reverse the scenario, however, and you have a glimpse of the awkward and often fraught transition that military new hires face.[10]

Consider this common scenario: A career service member—let's call him Steve—joins a civilian organization and, among other things, observes an environment in which people watch the clock and leave at the end of their shift whether the work got done or not, or who have strict boundaries around hours they will and won't work or days of the week they will and won't work. These are all very new concepts to Steve, coming from an environment in which the norm is to do whatever is needed, whenever it is needed, to accomplish a task or mission. Steve looks upon this civilian environment and thinks, "Wow, what a bunch of slackers. I'm going to have to bring some order to this place." Here's how some of our real interview subjects responded:

"I had let go of the expectation that I would be respected based on role/title. The employee attitude was, 'you can make me work but you can't make me work hard.'"

—ENLISTED SERVICE MEMBER, US NAVY[11]

"The biggest challenge was working with civilians who were more relaxed. A 40-hour week was half of my previous job in the military. There appeared to be no urgency to decision-making. The mindset was an adjustment."

—ENLISTED SERVICE MEMBER, US ARMY[12]

So begins the first culture clash, which is bound to aggravate all concerned. The clash is based on *a fundamental misunderstanding that civilian culture is similar to military culture.* Service members won't know a lot about this because they haven't yet discovered it. Therefore, the civilian employer must be the one to understand and anticipate the cultural differences so that you can effectively set and manage expectations from the earliest days of employment (in fact, before employment—during the recruitment process). This should be a two-way dialogue in which both parties voice their expectations and assumptions about what it means to do the job. It is only through such dialogue that core misunderstandings are revealed and, when it works, both parties learn from the exchange. The person quoted above is an Army sergeant. Interestingly, he demonstrated his own growing awareness with this advice to fellow transitioning service members:

> "Remember that you are not in uniform anymore. You are not a platoon sergeant with 65 people looking at you, afraid to move until you say jump. If you don't remember this, you will not make it because you will be a Type A unpleasant personality that everyone wants to get rid of!"

Military Culture

Veterans are unique because of the military's specific culture. This should not in any way be viewed as a negative. Approximately two hundred thousand service members transition to veteran status each year, according to the Department of Veterans Affairs. Of the many who continue to work, they will likely start new careers in the civilian workforce, whether in the private sector or government. Onboarding and engaging these employees provide some unique challenges and opportunities for organizations.

Think about the concept of boot camp. Not only is it a familiar term among civilians, it is part of our lexicon that suggests intensive training and/or indoctrination. Every military service member—active or veteran—has gone through some form of rigorous training, most often boot camp.* Because the military's mission requires great personal sacrifice, the culture must be regimented and unambiguous. There are established ways of doing things and standard operating procedures and infrastructure to ensure they are consistently observed. There are absolute norms and expectations about worthiness, professionalism, and subordination, among other things. Lives are at stake and the risks are too high for anything less than full compliance. Boot camp integrates these absolutes into automatic responses, creating a sense of communal responsibility and an "all for one and one for all" attitude. This is very different from the civilian workplace, which to veterans can look like "*me* for me and *you* for me." In the words of one former Army officer: "In the military you expect to go to work and see your friends. You look to the left and look to the right and see family. In civilian organizations, you look left and right and they're thinking about working their 8-hour shift and going home. They don't care about you."

The manner in which work is accomplished is also strikingly different in civilian organizations compared to the military. For example, many veterans observe that *how* work is accomplished can be as important to civilian employers as—maybe even more important than—*what* is being accomplished. This is counterintuitive to those coming from a mission-driven culture such as the military. Furthermore, many veterans find it distasteful. This can have an impact on a veteran's level of engagement with their civilian employer because it tugs at personal values regarding good uses of time and activity.

---

* Boot camp is for enlisted personnel, while officers attend another program called officer candidate school (OCS).

The Root of the Issue: Why Do These Cultural Differences Exist?

Organizational Mission

The discussion of cultural differences between the military and civilian workplace must begin with a discussion of mission. Mission dictates military culture; after all, the military has the most compelling of missions: protecting the nation and its allies. The fact that each and every member knows and is committed to this mission drives everything about the organization's culture. The culture *has* to support the mission because of what is at stake.

> "In the military, mission always comes first. You definitely try to take care of your people, but it's always, 'get the mission done regardless of the impact to the people.' For some folks in the military, that actually means putting people's lives at risk that work for you. What I have found in this [civilian] world is, mission is important but it's not always number one. It's more important that you look at the long view, even at some points of not accomplishing your mission. It's kind of losing a battle but still winning the war. That's the biggest difference I saw and the biggest challenge."
>
> —OFFICER, USAF[13]

In the military, "mission" means something tangible and specific. For example, the mission of the U.S. Air Force is to fly, fight, and win anytime, anywhere. These few words capture what the organization is there to do, how it will be accomplished, and where. All other tasks and activities are informed by this mission. It is a touchstone.

Military Mission Statements

U.S. Army

The U.S. Army's mission is to fight and win our Nation's wars by providing prompt, sustained land dominance across the full range of military operations and spectrum of conflict in support of combatant commanders.

U.S. Navy

The mission of the Navy is to maintain, train, and equip combat-ready Naval forces capable of winning wars, deterring aggression, and maintaining freedom of the seas.

U.S. Air Force

The mission of the U.S. Air Force is to fly, fight and win—airpower anytime, anywhere.

U.S. Marines

United States Marines are a family bound by a single purpose: the protection of our Nation and the advancement of its ideals.

U.S. Coast Guard

The mission of the United States Coast Guard is to ensure our Nation's maritime safety, security and stewardship.

U.S. Space Force

Our mission is to secure our Nation's interests in, from, and to space.

After reading the military mission statements, you may recognize some similarity to those of nonprofits, cause-related organizations, and some government entities.

Here are a few examples of nonprofit mission statements:

To enhance the quality of life in our City by working in partnership with the community and in accordance with constitutional rights to enforce the laws, preserve the peace, reduce fear, and provide for a safe environment.

To improve the quality of life through a balance between technology and nature.

To serve equally our members, our profession, and the public by defending liberty and delivering justice as the national representative of the legal profession.

For the most part, these mission statements clearly identify beneficiaries as populations in need of their services, not unlike the military. Something else they share with the military is a core value usually shared by everyone who works there. To be successful and effective, employees need to personally believe in the work that is being done. Otherwise, who would do it? These jobs are incredibly challenging for a variety of reasons, and it is often the deep connection to mission that motivates people to do them.

That said, a transition from the military to a nonprofit is not without its challenges, as illustrated by this recently retired USMC officer:

"Note the mission of my previous job: 'The mission of the rifle squad is to locate, close with, and destroy the enemy by fire and maneuver, or repel the enemy's assault by fire and close combat.' And now the mission of my current job in hospital administration, 'To improve the health of those we serve in a spirit of love and compassion.' The two missions are completely on opposite sides of the spectrum, but the dedication and values instilled in the armed forces are the same ones that mean so much to an organization, particularly one involved in healthcare."[14]

In contrast, while many businesses pride themselves on their values and service orientation, the main objective is to make a profit so they can stay in business. As a result, business culture is different and its mission statements tend to be less concrete and more multipurposed. They might accurately reflect the employee and customer experience—or they might not. They might be familiar and useful to employees and customers—or they might not.

Business mission statements generally include a purpose and an aim, a listing of primary stakeholders such as clients and shareholders, the organization's responsibilities toward these stakeholders, and something about the products and services offered. Some business mission statements are simple enough to be understood by all. Others are purposely abstract and open to multiple interpretations. Ultimately, though, regardless of the words on a page, the mission of a business is to stay in business, and this occurs through profit. This is the meta-mission that drives business culture whether or not it is specified in the official mission statement.

When you work for a for-profit organization, the profit part of the mission is assumed as a matter of course. Certainly it is the desire of most businesses to strive for loyalty and commitment among staff. But in the for-profit world it may be harder to engage employees with the mission, which can seem abstract and irrelevant. Company profit, even if linked to employee salary, is a vague concept that doesn't always produce passionate dedication from workers on the ground. As a result, personal commitment among employees is inconsistent in the business world. This often comes as a troubling surprise to service members who come from a world that values morale as a key component of success.

Of course, a CEO would want each and every employee to have a personal commitment to the company. In fact, large companies spend lots of money on programs, events, and "swag" (stuff we all get) to encourage loyalty and commitment among employees. Compared to the military, the corporate world relies much more on extrinsic rewards such as bonuses, perks, and merit raises. Senior executives often have the drive to accomplish financial goals, but for the average worker, profit alone is tough to get excited about. In contrast, the military has the intrinsic rewards of service, patriotism, and protecting the nation.

I developed a model to illustrate how an organization's mission shapes its culture, operations, and day-to-day behavior. Presented in two parts, the model looks first at the military mission and culture, then at the civilian organization's mission and culture. The term "Observable Characteristics" refers to easily observed aspects of an organization's true culture, what you and I could point to as typical of the organization based on what we observe about it. Let's begin with the military.

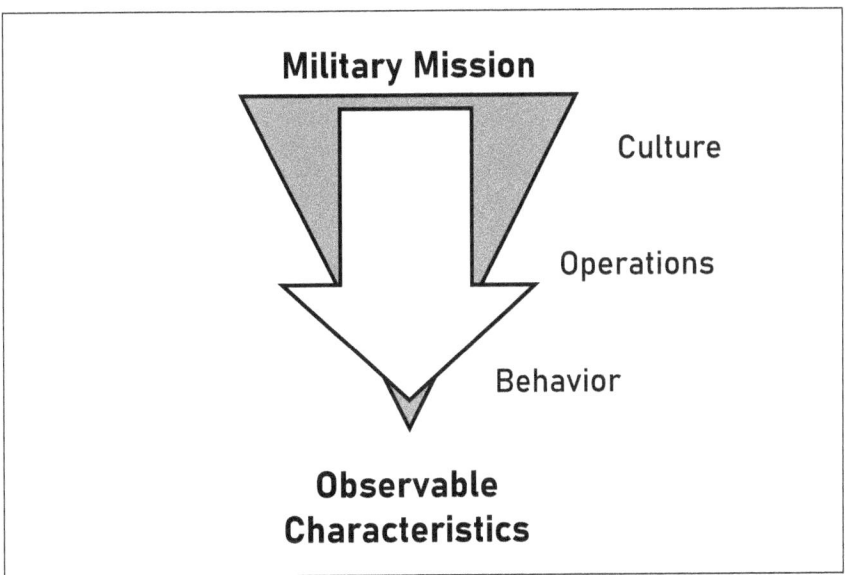

In the military, the mission is at the broadest part of the triangle. Mission sits on top of everything else, and everything falls out of an understanding and commitment to that mission. As the triangle narrows, the mission is concentrating through the organization and shaping behavior, events, practices, and processes to the point where almost anybody could rattle off a couple of stereotypical military characteristics like "hierarchical," or "formal," or "directive."

That's what the military mission requires. In order for people to succeed in that complex environment, everyone needs to be crystal clear about the mission, to the point that it is infused in every single thing they do.

Now, let's compare this to the civilian organizational structure:

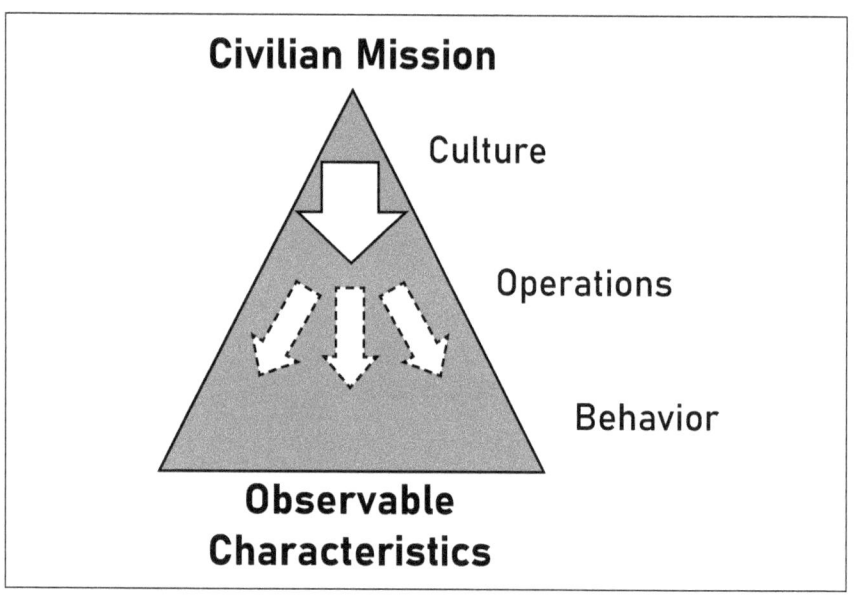

Looking now at the second triangle, we see the narrowest point at the top and the wide plane at its base. This represents civilian organizational culture where the mission still resides at the top but, unlike military culture, it teeters on an unstable point. The base of the triangle represents observable cultural characteristics. Unlike the military's approach to mission, in a civilian organization a mission may be just words on a page. It may be the output of a leadership exercise intended to inspire and guide. It may be hung on walls around the office, embedded into policies and norms, or not.

As the triangle broadens toward the base, the mission can become diffuse. Fewer people may be able to recite the mission statement. Some might not even know what it is or that it exists. In fact, it is not unusual in the civilian workplace to find policies and practices in place that actually undermine the stated mission.

Bottom line: behavior that an outside observer could see and name is highly individualized in most civilian organizations. The extent to which any employee embodies the mission of the organization will vary widely. Typically the more senior one's role in the organization, the closer one is to the mission in terms of understanding goals and how to drive desired outcomes. That perspective tends to diffuse as you move down through the organization. Here's how one former Army officer described it:

"On the operational side, you get a task. You finish it. You move on to the next task. You are in a comfort zone: 'I know the guy on the left and the guy on the right of me all had the same training. Our expectations are all pretty much the same in achieving a goal.' I get on the corporate side, I don't have that warm fuzzy of 'does the guy at the top to the guy at the bottom have the same goals for the company or the unit as a whole?' And are we going to get there in the same way? I don't know everybody's backgrounds and schooling, what they know, what they provide, and what value they bring."[15]

To fully grasp the contrast between these two illustrations of culture, let's view them side by side:

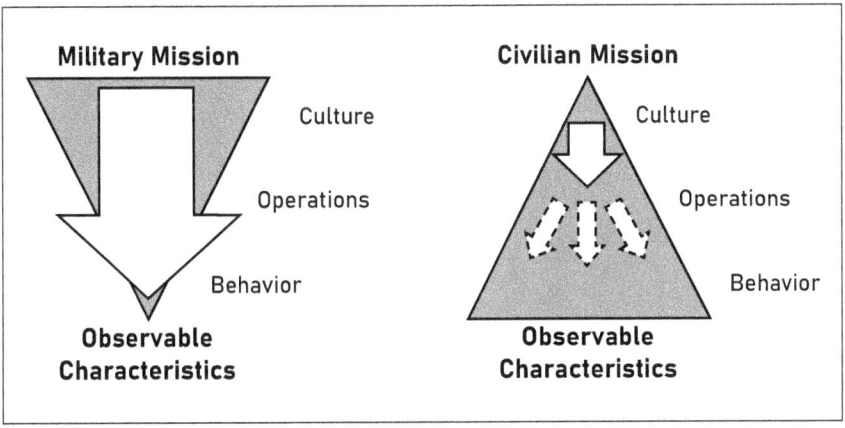

Employers: Remember the scenario earlier in the chapter in which you were dropped into a military job after a successful career as a civilian HR professional? You left an organization whose mission may or may not have played a role in day-to-day operations, as illustrated by the pointy tip of the civilian triangle above. You entered the military environment unaware of the wide flat plane of mission you now stood upon. Can you see how this basic lack of organizational context led to some of the missteps you made on your very first day? The military mission is served by the hierarchy of its rank structure and the expectations of deference and respect that go along with it. Things that may seem like trivial niceties in your civilian career—like how you sign an email—can, in the military, actually be barriers to accomplishing your assigned task because they disrupt the culture.

Military service members transitioning into civilian work environments experience a disorientation similar to what you would experience if you were dropped into the rigid structure of their environment. Here's how one former enlisted service member described it:

"The chain of command is circumvented in civilian culture; elevating things above the boss, not respecting the boss. The impact is a breakdown in morale, in communication, and team unity."[16]

Veterans come to the civilian workplace with an expectation that mission will be first, that they will stand upon a wide plane of mission-first culture. Sooner or later they come to the same realization you did in the earlier scenario: the basic assumption about what's important is inaccurate. Actions taken under this wrong assumption will, necessarily, rock the boat to some extent. Veterans can interpret this disconnection from mission as a lack of integrity on the part of the civilian organization.

As an officer in the U.S. Army says, "Mission has to be broadcast all the way down to the janitor and, in the military, it is. On the other hand, I've had civilian managers say, 'Don't worry about all that. Just focus on what you're supposed to be doing right now.'"[17]

Navigating the Journey: How to Address Cultural Challenges

Culture and Organizational Context

Compared to the military, many civilian organizations appear to have a loose structure that can look uncoordinated or even chaotic. Military service members are trained to bring order to chaos. How? By imposing command-and-control leadership. After all, in the military, "chaos" can look like last-minute deployments or operations requiring people to stop everything and completely redirect their attention and activity. Chaos in a corporate setting looks more like missed deadlines, unavailable clients, no time to prepare for a key meeting, staff away on leave, a messy desk, etc. Impose a command-and-control leadership style on this scenario and you may well see a spike in attrition!

The stakes are different. The competitive nature of the market requires agility in the form of changes to organization structure. You don't see that happening in the military. The military is what it is. It's got a structure that works for its mission and it stays true to that. So a common point of frustration about civilian organizations is, for many veterans, an apparent absence of leadership. For example, processes may not be consistently documented; people seem to be using any number of approaches to accomplish the same task, and with different quality standards. Some people don't even seem to know what the larger goal is of the work that they're doing. Corporate restructuring is common in civilian organizations, but can look ill-conceived and arbitrary to the veteran, as if nobody really knows what they're doing.

Without the benefit of a *cultural translator*, someone who understands both cultures and can speak in both contexts, the service member may not understand in practical terms that civilian organizations need to be flexible, especially in a for-profit environment, and that learning occurs in real time, with real cost and risk associated with it. Certainly business strives to be proactive in anticipation of market shifts, but the reality is that business responds to market needs, and market needs are constantly changing. That's why organizations change their structures one, two, three times or more. They do whatever it takes to meet market demands.

Failing to comprehend the vastly different organizational context of a civilian organization sets a military new hire up for disappointment right out of the gate. Time and again, I see this disappointment, even disillusionment, misattributed to the hiring organization when it should be attributed to the civilian workplace at large. The misattribution results in attrition and can be easily corrected by early education and expectation-setting on the part of the employer.

For example, a veteran leaves company A to go to company B, where the pastures are greener. Upon arrival he finds that some of the things he disliked about the first civilian employer are present in the second civilian organization, and maybe a third. It can take that third job change before the veteran sees himself as the common denominator in the equation. This can be an "aha" moment, or it can pass without notice. Regardless, it is at this point that the tacit learning accumulated from the previous organizations kicks in, along with a recalibration of expectations that is more realistic and accepting. For example, what previously looked like a lack of values may now be understood as market agility. What looked like self-interest on the part of employees may now look like the challenge of balancing work with personal goals and priorities. What looked like a lack of leadership may now look like the complexity of managing in a changing environment.

A smart organization anticipates the risk of misattribution and sees the imperative to communicate organizational context early in the veteran's new-hire experience. Any investment of time and resources will pay dividends in the form of accelerated performance and, one hopes, retention over time.

I recommend providing some level of transition support that doesn't have the company's footprint on it *before* sending the service member to standard new-hire orientation. For example, such support could include discussion of common success factors and pitfalls associated with moving from a military to civilian work environment, how to think about and prioritize around organizational mission, and basics of interpersonal norms in civilian culture.

The reality is that this support does not exist for most service members. The military doesn't provide it, and most employers don't either (often it is out of reach for midsize and small organizations). Yet the need is very real. So, my company, Grandinetta Group, has created it. The Accelerated Military Transition Course is recommended for all military branches, ranks, and occupations. We believe it to be the very best solution to the military-civilian divide.

The timing matters because without some basics regarding the civilian workplace, organization-specific training is completely abstract and disconnected for the veteran. Return for a moment to the previous scenario in which you joined the military in late career. How helpful would an orientation to your new HR department have been without first being oriented to the military?

> "The hardest part [of the transition] was deciding what to wear in the morning. After 20 years of knowing how to put on a uniform, dressing for the corporate world was a challenge!"
>
> —ENLISTED SERVICE MEMBER, USAF[18]

Lest you hear this statement in a negative context (e.g., downplaying the challenge of transition), see this comment from another former service member:

> "I would like to add one more piece of advice to the transitioning personnel. … Ensure that their wardrobe is updated and that they have at least two good suits. Otherwise, they will be scrambling to try and put together a wardrobe at the last minute and also probably have to pay out a lot of money."
>
> —ENLISTED SERVICE MEMBER, USMC[19]

Clearly, this concern is very real!

Career civilians don't need this "basic training" because they've picked it up over the course of previous work experiences. Other things an organization can offer its employees who served in the military are awareness training for recruiters, line managers, and human resource professionals; individual and small-group mentoring; and self-study resources. This will be discussed further in Part 3 of the book.

The following worksheet was developed for a veteran transition program we developed for a large consultancy. The version below provides insight into the military new hire's experience. Let's examine some typical responses to questions about the transition process:

Life Out of Uniform

When I wore my uniform I felt *comfortable, part of a community, didn't have to always introduce myself because people could see by my uniform how to act and I knew how to act based on theirs.*

When I returned it at the end of my service, I felt *free at first, then a little lost. Felt like a loss of status.*

How do I communicate who I am now, without the uniform? *Have to start over with every new person, takes longer, funny to see how people's tone changes when they finally figure out you outrank them!*

How do I identify who others are now, in a world without uniforms? *No clue! At first you try to figure it out by what they're wearing, but that is useless. Then you try to hear what people call them, but that doesn't work because, around here, everyone goes by their first name. Basically, I just try not to make any assumptions and wait to be introduced. Hopefully that will tell me something about who the other person is in relation to me!*

What tips would you give newly separated service members? *Just hang in there, you'll figure it out eventually! Just try not to offend anyone in the meantime!*

There is humor and humility in the responses provided on this veteran's worksheet. This is a great posture to assume when making the military transition, as it makes learning easier than when we assume a resistant stance. We'll talk more about this in Part 2 of the book.

I use a metaphor based on sunglasses with my military clients preparing to transition into civilian employment, and it seems to help manage expectations. "Along with turning in your uniform, you also need to return the military-issued 'sunglasses.' You will be given a new pair by your civilian employer. Initially they may not work well because you're used to looking through the other pair of shades; things may look blurry, out of focus, you may even stumble around a bit. Expect that challenge and take it on with a spirit of curiosity."

Practical Application:

Coaching Conversation

To illustrate how cultural differences manifest in the workplace, consider the following exchange between veteran new-hire Liz and her manager. In this scenario, Liz is seeking advice from her manager about staff management.

Coaching Conversation: Cultural Challenge

Liz: Thanks for your time today. I could really use your advice on a staff management issue I'm struggling with.

Manager: Sure thing, Liz. What's going on? [How would you describe your current performance challenge?]

Liz: I just can't seem to get used to how staff interact with managers in this environment. They have no problem coming right into my office with complaints or suggestions.

Manager: What have you tried so far to address the challenge?

Liz: Well, it didn't take long to see that reprimanding them for insubordination did not work. After that mistake, which I won't make again, I haven't really known what to do except listen and promise to take their issue under advisement.

Manager: How effective was that approach?

Liz: One person just kept bugging me about it until I lost my patience and barked at her. I just can't seem to get used to the lack of respect shown to superiors.

Manager: How is it similar to situations you faced in the military?

Liz: It isn't. It would never happen in the military.

Manager: How is it different here compared to the military?

Liz: Well, here, people have free will to quit if they want to. So if they are valuable employees, they kind of have you over a barrel. You, as manager, have no choice but to keep them happy, even if it means the job doesn't get done.

Manager: What have you observed others doing in response to similar challenges in this environment?

[pause]

Liz: I watch my peers, who seem to do a lot of compromising and accommodating of staff.

Manager: How effective is that approach?

Liz: It definitely defuses the situation if the employee is emotional. It also makes more work for the manager, though.

Manager: What could you do to more effectively address the challenge?

Liz: I would like to find a way to deal with it that doesn't necessarily add to my workload, but that encourages the employee to be part of the solution rather than just handing it off.

Manager: How would you see that playing out?

Liz: Good question! I think that after listening to the employee describe the issue and confirming that I understand it correctly, I could start by asking him or her for suggestions as to how they could address it. Or, like you just asked me, I could ask what they've already done to address it. That would train them to try to resolve it before coming to me in the future. And I could wrap up by asking what, if anything, they want to request of me in terms of assistance. How does that approach sound to you?

Manager: I think it sounds great. I use a similar approach with my direct reports so they try to resolve their own issues before elevating them to me, while knowing they'll have my support if they need it. So, what's the next step?

Liz: One of the analysts is on my calendar this afternoon to discuss an issue. I want to jot down some notes beforehand to remind myself of what to say, then I'm going to put it to work and see how it goes. Thanks!

Moving Forward: Action Steps for Success

One of the most powerful tools for helping service members accelerate their cultural learning curve is the ability to clearly translate your organization's culture into concrete meaning. For example, it might be self-evident that "teamwork" refers to working collaboratively, helping coworkers, and working together toward a shared goal. I'm sure it has greater nuance in your organization's unique culture. But in the military, "teamwork" can have additional connotations, such as doing whatever it takes to get a task done, including working around the clock and expecting everyone else to do the same. In the civilian world of budget constraints, billability requirements, employment/work requirements, operational costs, and work-life balance, this may not be a realistic approach.

Generally speaking, we aren't aware of all of the assumptions we make about what other people know or don't know—especially regarding things we consider to be obvious. As a result, key misunderstandings or misinterpretations only come to light after a mistake has been made. This can be a costly way of uncovering assumptions. To combat this, you as a leader in your organization need to perfect the skill of translating culture so it can be explained before mistakes are made. The good news is that I have developed a translator tool to help you make the implicit explicit by breaking down words, phrases, and concepts into behavioral terms. There are four steps to using the translator tool:

1. Select a *word or concept* used by your organization.
2. Interpret the word or concept according to its *practical meaning*.
3. Further break down the word or concept into *concrete behaviors* that exemplify it.
4. Articulate the organization's formal or stated *expectations*.

The translator tool below is an example, based on the concept of teamwork used earlier.

Now these are not textbook definitions and may bear little or no resemblance to how teamwork is thought of or measured by your organization. That is not important. What is important is to connect the dots between words a veteran is likely to hear and expected behaviors. Your ability to connect these dots will have a very real impact on how long it takes new hires to adapt and perform effectively in your organization's culture.

The practical application for employers below has room for you to insert words or terms commonly used in your organization.

Remember to use the translator tool to help articulate and support standards of leadership, and translate them for incoming military hires. Practice using it below:

1. Start with the word "leadership" as it is used in your organization.
2. Interpret "leadership" according to its *practical meaning*.
3. Further break down the word "leadership" into *concrete behaviors* that exemplify it.
4. Articulate the organization's formal or stated *expectations* for leadership.

Here's an example using the concept of "teamwork":

Translator Tool: Corporate Sample

Word/concept: Teamwork

Practical meaning: work collaboratively with peers & colleagues

Concrete behavior(s): share information, be inclusive so that anyone & everyone who might be impacted by your work is in the communication loop, be willing to help others & to ask for help from others, avoid finger-pointing & blame when things go wrong.

Formal expectation(s): the organization measures employees on the following competencies related to teamwork: demonstration of helpfulness, ability to work cross-functionally, ability to work flexibly and adapt to changing work requirements.

Practical Application for Employers: Using the Translator Tool

---

Now that we've explored the importance of translating cultural expectations, it's time to apply this knowledge to your own organization. Use the following exercise to practice using the translator tool with common terms in your workplace.

Instructions:

1. Choose a word or concept commonly used in your organization.
2. Fill in the practical meaning as understood in your workplace.
3. List concrete behaviors that demonstrate this concept in action.
4. Describe any formal expectations or measurements related to this concept in your organization.

EXAMPLE

Word/concept: Teamwork

Practical Meaning: Working with others to execute tasks

Concrete Behavior(s): Making your calendar visible to the team, consulting with them on timelines before making them public, working through disagreements constructively so that relationships remain intact

Formal Expectation(s): [insert official language here; may be found in documented values or competencies]

* * *

Now you try!

Word/concept:

Practical Meaning:

Concrete Behavior(s):

Formal Expectation(s):

By completing this exercise, you'll be better equipped to communicate cultural expectations to new hires, especially those transitioning from military service. This practice can help prevent misunderstandings and smooth the onboarding process for veterans joining your team.

Closing Thoughts

It's so easy to take meanings for granted, to assume things are obvious and forget what it was like to be a newcomer. When we take a moment to see our organization through the eyes of a new hire, we see more, but it still takes intention and effort to ensure mutual understanding of cultural norms and the everyday shorthand we use to communicate with colleagues. Raising your awareness of this common blind spot will help you remember to be clear, and to position veteran new hires for early success and accelerated learning in your organization.

Current and former service members reading this chapter: Your key takeaway is that even the simplest words can be interpreted very differently outside the military. Be curious and, when in doubt, ask! For example, if a civilian interviewer says, "We expect all new employees to be collaborative from day one," you want to follow that up with something like, "To avoid an assumption based on my military experience, could you please share how your organization thinks about being collaborative. How does 'collaborative' look in your organization? What would tell you someone was or wasn't being collaborative from day one?"

Remember to be curious!

Chapter 4

Common Challenges of Military Transition

"Veterans are leaving an extremely regimented world for a [civilian] world where they have a voice, and commanding everyone is not necessary or accepted. There will be a definite need for molding and counseling during this adjustment, but their dedication, diligence, and determination to achieving the goal is worth it."

—ENLISTED SERVICE MEMBER, US ARMY[20]

Understanding the Landscape: What Challenges Do Veterans Face in Transition?

ALONG WITH THE UNIQUE STRENGTHS that veterans bring with them to the civilian workplace, there is a complementary set of shared challenges. Most of the challenges relate to the transition itself and can therefore be anticipated and addressed early on.

I have found the cultural learning curve to be the biggest challenge and the primary differentiator between those who successfully transition to civilian careers and those who struggle to find success. In fact, research has shown that the cultural learning curve to transition into a new organization can take twice as long for veterans as it does for civilians. Being on this learning curve doesn't mean the veteran isn't productive; to the contrary, quickly adding value is important to many veterans and, without savvy managers, they may spend a great deal of time trying to figure things out on their own. What the learning curve means is that the nuances of civilian operations and interaction take longer to master.

Based on extensive work with transitioning service members, I have identified four specific challenges that are common to former service members as they enter civilian organizations. These challenges are organizational context, interpersonal style, management/leadership philosophy, and tolerating ambiguity.

The Root of the Issue: Why Do These Differences Matter?

The key to accelerating the learning curve is a strong manager or mentor who takes time to understand and anticipate challenges veterans are likely to encounter.

One example of a cultural nuance that has tripped up more than a few veterans has to do with communicating about salary and earnings. The military pay structure is transparent and uniform (pun not really intended!), so talking and commiserating about pay is pretty common. There is nothing taboo about it in that culture. However, in the civilian workplace, it is often frowned upon and may even be a violation of policy to disclose salary information to colleagues or discuss perceived inequities. The lack of transparency in the civilian workplace often comes as a strange surprise to veterans, and can be interpreted as a lack of basic fairness and integrity. This fundamental lack of understanding can create needless noise and unhappiness, yet is relatively simple to rectify by describing cultural norms early in the employment process.

Another salient example of a cultural nuance is the notion of leadership. The military is known for developing leaders, and no one does it like the military. It provides opportunities and training for leadership that far exceed what many civilian managers and leaders receive. Accordingly, civilian organizations often seek out former service members for their leadership skills. *What most fail to consider is that these leadership skills were developed in the military context, which may not exactly fit their organization's culture.* Therefore, unless your organization's culture is characterized by a command-and-control style of leadership, the leadership experience of veterans will need some modification. For many, this is accomplished with time and feedback. For others, it takes longer to appreciate the validity of other approaches and to pick up on cultural nuances related to how leadership is expressed. In the words of one retired USAF officer:

> "The military is very rank-structured. You are respected just outright because you wear the rank. People don't know you from Adam, but they see the rank on your shoulders and you get respect automatically because of that. In the [civilian] world, that's not the case. Nobody knows your rank. You have to build that respect and trust."[21]

Navigating the Journey: Top Challenges and How to Address Them

Let's examine these four key challenges in more detail:

1. Adapting to organizational context. Military and civilian organizations exist in different organizational contexts. The term refers to internal and external factors that influence the organization such as those illustrated in the following table:

Examples of Organizational Context

Internal Factors	External Factors
Structure (e.g., government agency, privately held or publicly traded company, nonprofit)	**Economic Conditions** (e.g., impacted by recession vs. recession-proof, consumer spending, unemployment rate, talent shortage)
Culture (e.g., formal, informal, regulated, unregulated, innovative, risk averse, mission driven, profit driven, safety focused)	**Market Trends** (e.g., technology advances, demand for innovation, industry disruptors, consumer preferences)
Resources (e.g., funding source, budget constraints, investment in people or technology)	**Regulatory/Legal Changes** (e.g., Congressional mandates, environmental regulations, degree of government oversight)
Stakeholders (e.g., owners, investors, employees, customers, shareholders, partners, agencies)	**Social/Cultural Shifts** (e.g., emphasis on diversity, generational trends, political sentiment)

For example, veterans have not worked in a context where their time and output had a dollar amount associated with it. Consider the former officer, now a consultant, whose time is billed at $500 per hour but who spends an hour trying to clear a printer jam because "someone's got to do it." The whatever-it-takes attitude is great, and all employees could take a lesson from his example, but it is also misapplied in this case because the value of the hour spent with the printer equates to $500 for the company. Perhaps the jam could have been taken care of by someone whose role had low or no cost impact. The point is that veterans come into the business world with a set of definitions around time and money that may not apply in a business context where profit and time are closely related.

Another and perhaps more significant change of context for the veteran is coming into a civilian world where employment is voluntary. They now work alongside people who can quit any time they want, or be asked to leave, and they're managing staff who can quit if they don't like the way they're being treated. Think back to the discussion of command-and-control leadership on the previous pages. Not only does the approach keep things moving forward in the military, but it is also unquestioned because employment is contractual. Service members can't just walk off the job because they dislike their officers. In the words of one enlisted member of the Navy:

> "I was surprised at the amount of personal freedom given to the employee on the civilian side. I had to adjust my working style and organizational skills to a world that required self-starters to be successful."[22]

2. Modifying interpersonal style. You've probably experienced firsthand the difference between what someone says and how they say it. It is easy to misinterpret the content if it is delivered in a manner that is off-putting or raises defenses. In the civilian workplace, interpersonal style can be the difference between gaining the support of peers and alienating them, between motivating staff and intimidating them, between influencing senior executives and clamming up out of deference to authority. Interpersonal styles can be as diverse as the individuals in the organization.

The military, by contrast, ingrains an interpersonal style that supports its mission. The communication style is often described as terse, impersonal, and direct, because the mission of the military requires communication to be fast and clear. To acknowledge something someone has said, it is perfectly acceptable to say "check" or "noted." Those one-word acknowledgments are often perceived by civilians as dismissive. Feeling dismissed can quickly lead to a misinterpretation of meaning and intention, which in turn can damage relationships. Ironically, the attempt to be clear and direct actually creates a lack of clarity regarding intent. A civilian might think, "I just walked up to the new guy's office door and informed him of a meeting this afternoon. He said, 'check.' What is that? Are we computers now?"

If your organization wants to integrate veterans into its culture, the solution is twofold: first, describe the organization's style of interacting and communicating during the onboarding process and, second, raise awareness among all employees of the military context. Many large organizations do this under the auspices of diversity, equity, and inclusion. Viewing it as such encourages everyone to be more effective, not just in the way they say things but in the meaning they choose to attach to what others say to them. Simple awareness training can head off a host of day-to-day misunderstandings.

3. Acclimating to management and leadership approach. Veterans and their employers experience a disconnect when it comes to expectations of leadership. Both know the word "leadership" but have very different definitions and expectations of how it looks in day-to-day operation. This disconnect can create problems on both sides, in the form of perceived failure to meet expectations. For example, the veteran may feel misled in the interview process. "They said the company offers leadership training, but there are no good leaders there and no accountability." Meanwhile, the employer feels misled as well. "The résumé was full of leadership experience but the style doesn't work for us. Issuing terse directives to others and expecting respect based on job title is not what we need here."

In the military, the leadership philosophy and approach evolve directly from the mission. Leadership is trained and expected from Day One. It has specific boundaries and activities associated with it, a clear protocol for accomplishing a clear mission. The organization is designed to develop leaders. In this context, it's relatively straightforward to understand why things are done the way they are once you grasp the mission.

In civilian organizations, it may be harder to clarify the mission itself, let alone the leadership philosophy. Civilian leaders may or may not receive training. Leadership roles are often earned on the basis of measurable performance over time. The lack of standardized training, philosophy, and role definition in civilian environments means leadership can look an infinite number of ways, none of which may be recognizable as leadership to a veteran.

4. Tolerating ambiguity. Certainly the military has its share of ambiguity, as any organization its size does. But the ambiguity veterans find in civilian settings often appears to them as a lack of leadership. The ambiguity they are accustomed to tolerating in the military is what I would call "controlled ambiguity" because, yes, there may be ambiguity, but it exists in the context of this super-structured organization and culture in which there are ways of doing things that are documented and followed. In the military, the point is to limit the degree of ambiguity associated with change by executing change in a stable and prescribed manner. For example, veterans I've worked with tended to brush off the significance of military transition because, in service, they've had to change duties/roles/location every three years. While this does require adaptivity, the cadence is predictable and the operational setup is similar from base to base. This is intentional, to limit the time and disruption associated with these rotations.

In contrast, ambiguity in the civilian workplace can manifest anywhere, at any time, in any form, and by anyone, and is often experienced by a veteran as chaos. "Why isn't anybody in charge around here?" and "How does this place stay in business, changing their strategy every year?" are common questions asked by military new hires. And they may be fair questions. But they do not lead to insight or discovery; they simply accuse. Asking (or even just thinking) questions in an accusatory manner is not conducive to success for most new hires, military or not. Commercial organizations must be agile to stay competitive, which means employees must be agile.

This again is an issue of expectation-setting, which should begin during recruitment and continue through onboarding. It is about setting clear expectations that are accurate, that don't make assumptions about what the veteran knows, and that paint a clear picture of what the veteran is going to be walking into and how daily life might be a little (or a lot) different than it was in the military.

Moving Forward: Action Steps for Success

Strategies for Employers and Veterans

To foster mutual success, both employers and veterans need to approach this difference with open eyes and minds before committing to one another. To bridge this gap, both veterans and employers need to take proactive steps:

EMPLOYERS

Ask yourselves: "What is my organization's leadership philosophy? Is it mission first? People first? Profit first? How does this philosophy manifest in our daily operations?" A disconnect between stated values and actual practices will be quickly evident to veterans, so it's crucial to avoid a breach of trust early on. Consider these questions:

- How does your organization think about leadership?
- To what extent are these beliefs an abstract philosophy and to what extent are they actually practiced? What are some examples?
- If you were to ask yourself why managers and leaders do what they do, would you say it was to serve the organization's mission? To avoid repercussions? To keep the boss happy? To keep staff happy? To take the path of least resistance?

Taking time to reflect on your organization's leadership philosophy (whether it is formally articulated or not) will help you explain context to your military hires. They will come in expecting leadership to be focused on mission, and they may disengage if they sense that leadership is focused on politics, self-interest, or other goals not directly related to mission. Explaining this context will help to set realistic expectations among new hires.

Throughout my years working with organizations and former military service members, I've observed that when veterans can navigate the learning curve of applying their management and leadership skills in a civilian setting, they often become outstanding leaders who are respected, enjoyed, and even beloved. However, this adaptation process may require coaching, either through the onboarding process or in dedicated leadership training.

VETERANS

Prepare for a significant shift in leadership culture. This is going to be different for you and may feel like a collective failure to lead. Many veterans quickly assess and declare their new civilian organization to be wrong, bad, lacking, chaotic, unfixable. Your challenge here is to suspend judgment. Recognize that the business context is substantially different from the military context, and approach your new role with humility. Your assumption needs to be that you know very little about why the organization operates as it does. After all, it is likely that the organization was doing just fine before you came along and will continue to do just fine if/after you leave. Your leadership skills and abilities will come into play over time; trust in this and be patient.

Closing Thoughts

While this chapter provides an overview of common transition challenges, you will find the topic of culture interwoven throughout every chapter that follows. Besides the often-reported feeling of loss of identity and community, the cultural difference between military life and civilian work is arguably the most challenging aspect of transition for both veterans and companies that employ them. Developing effective strategies for absorbing and addressing this challenge lies at the root of what I'd call the military-civilian divide. The following chapters offer enlightening concepts and practical tools designed to facilitate a smooth transition for all parties. By understanding and addressing these cultural differences, both veterans and employers can work together to create more successful and fulfilling career transitions.

Chapter 5

Military Transition as a Matter of Diversity, Equity & Inclusion (DEI)

"I think many lower enlisted personnel don't understand finances as well as they should for the civilian world. Many things in the military, such as healthcare, are taken care of for them. I think they should understand taxable income and how much comes from their paychecks to cover many of the benefits that were previously given to them."

—ENLISTED SERVICE MEMBER, US NAVY[23]

Understanding the Landscape: Why Is Military Transition a DEI Matter?

I SEE MILITARY-TO-CIVILIAN TRANSITION AS A DIVERSITY, EQUITY, AND INCLUSION MATTER. At the simplest level—demographically—veterans are a diverse group. A deeper look reveals even more compelling evidence of veterans as a diverse group. Specifically, veterans meet four key criteria that define a diverse population in the workforce:

1. They are a clearly defined group (i.e., it is possible to say whether one was or was not in the U.S. military).
2. They come from a strong, distinct culture.
3. They face a shared set of challenges in the civilian workforce.
4. Their military background can significantly impact their success as civilian employees, both positively and negatively.

The Impact of Self-Perception on Transition Success

Previously, I posted an article on my blog discussing why some veterans find the transition to civilian life easier than others. I referenced two examples, loosely based on clients I've worked with over the years.

Example 1: The Humble Learner

In the first case, the retired officer recognized he was leaving one world behind—the military—and entering a new world—the civilian world. He acknowledged knowing very little about how to succeed or thrive in the new work environment. So he came in humble, expecting to *feel* like a beginner for a while. With defenses down, he was receptive to learning.

Example 2: The Resistant Leader

The second example offered a useful contrast. Also a retired officer who had achieved a certain level of officer status and left service at the peak of his career, he too had a number of offers to consider from civilian organizations. In fact, he really felt like he was the "It" guy in the market. He proceeded with an attitude of "I'm at the top of my game and you're lucky to have me." He was not open to learning, he was defensive about feedback, and he had a rigid way of doing things that allowed for no alternative approach. The stressful situation of being a senior leader in a completely new work environment seemed to amplify the worst side of some characteristically military operating styles. The more resistance he got from his civilian staff (which would be insubordination in the military and not permitted), the more dug-in this gentleman became. Things spiraled down to the point where he had alienated himself from his peers. Staff didn't like him and were beginning to disengage. His superiors began to see him as a liability, unsure of his ability to make a successful transition into the civilian organization.

Outcomes

The humble learner in the first example quickly developed a fan base, experimented with being himself in an organization that didn't require regimented behavior, and was ultimately promoted to an even higher level of executive leadership. In contrast, the resistant leader in the second example was given probationary status and eventually chose to leave the organization.

Key Takeaway: Success in transition is a responsibility shared between the veteran and the organization. Organizations that understand the military context and provide resources to assist in the transition will be more likely to retain military talent. As one USAF enlisted member noted, "I knew I could contribute more, but didn't know how to plug in. I got lumped in with other military folks, but we are all individuals."[24]

In many organizations, there are designated teams or individuals responsible for supporting diverse populations. Veterans are a group that can benefit significantly from such diversity, equity, and inclusion initiatives.

The Root of the Issue: Why Some Struggle with Diversity

The Importance of Managing Assumptions

Individuals with civilian work experience accumulate tacit knowledge about business operations that veterans might lack. Examples include:

1. Time-tracking procedures
2. Choosing benefits plans
3. Salary negotiations
4. Submitting expense reports
5. Contributing to business profitability

As a new college graduate, I faced similar challenges, learning professional norms through trial and error. Unlike my situation, veterans may face additional hurdles in understanding workplace expectations. As a civilian line manager or HR professional, it is crucial to avoid assumptions about a veteran's knowledge of civilian workplace norms and instead provide explicit guidance. These assumptions can lead to problems such as performance breakdowns, communication gaps, poor working relationships, costs (both actual and opportunity), and high turnover, to name a few. Recognizing that everyone has a learning curve is an essential first step in addressing these challenges.

Addressing Personal Bias

Biases about veterans can stem from various sources, including political views, news coverage, and portrayal in movies. It's important for both veterans and civilian colleagues to be aware of their attitudes and potential biases. Organizations should encourage open dialogue and provide training to address these biases. Successfully integrating veterans into civilian workplaces requires effort from both the veterans and the organizations hiring them. By recognizing veterans as a diverse group, managing assumptions, and addressing biases, companies can create more inclusive environments that benefit from the unique skills and perspectives veterans bring to the table. This approach not only supports veterans in their transition but also enriches the overall diversity, equity, and inclusion of the workplace.

To better understand and address our biases, it can be helpful to examine them systematically. Consider the following example of an assumption check-in process:

Assumption Check-in: Corporate Example

Bias/Assumption/Stereotype: *Military veterans are rigid and inflexible.*

When/where did I learn this to be true? *Growing up, I had an uncle who made us do things a certain way, and it had to be just so; like if we borrowed his tools we had to put them back in the exact same place we took them from, and he would get really mad if we misplaced or left them out.*

Looking at it now, what evidence tells me it is, in fact, true? *I have met lots of military service members over the years who were like my uncle in this way.*

What evidence tells me that it may not be true? *I have met several veterans over the years who were easygoing and didn't care how something got done as long as it got done right.*

How can I check this out or learn more about it? *Notice the qualities of being rigid and inflexible wherever they may be, and pay attention to my tendency to assume veterans will operate this way. Ask if the person is open to other approaches and to negotiating.*

My updated view could be restated this way: *Being rigid and inflexible is not unique to military veterans. It is a work style I see in all kinds of people, and that I find personally challenging to deal with.*

My growth opportunity: *I can work on not being shut down by people who seem rigid and inflexible.*

This process isn't just for civilians examining their assumptions about veterans. It's equally important for veterans to examine their own assumptions about civilian life and work. Here's an example of how a veteran might use this process:

Assumption Check-in: Military Example

Bias/Assumption/Stereotype: *Military transition is not a concern; I've changed jobs and duty stations every three years for my entire career. Change doesn't scare me.*

When/where did I learn this to be true? *My only work experience has been in the military, and that means constant change and adaptation to new things. Why would this career change be any different?*

Looking at it now, what evidence tells me it is, in fact, true? *Everything is different. It's nothing like a change of duty station, and no one really prepares you for it. You have to ask a lot of questions.*

What evidence tells me that it may not be true? *I know how to do the job—or rather I know how we did it in the military. How they do it here is completely different and my instincts are not working. I am constantly corrected by my peers and even people junior to me. Why is this so hard?*

How can I check this out or learn more about it? *Acknowledge that military transition is a bit more complicated than a change of duty station. Ask about everything—even things you thought were obvious. Connect up with the veterans' Employee Resource Group to talk to others who have gone through this transition before me.*

My updated view could be restated this way: *This is not what I expected; I didn't expect to feel like a beginner at this stage of my life.*

My growth opportunity: *Check my ego; different isn't automatically wrong, and I am not incompetent. Use humility and humor to make the learning curve easier.*

Activity: Assumption Check-In

Bias/Assumption/Stereotype: _____

_____

When/where did I learn this to be true? _____

_____

Looking at it now, what evidence tells me it is, in fact, true? ___

_____

What evidence tells me that it may not be true?_____

_____

How can I check this out or learn more about it?_____

_____

My updated view could be restated this way:_____

_____

My growth opportunity: _____

_____

Closing Thoughts

Viewing veterans in the civilian workplace through the lens of diversity, equity, and inclusion enables organizations to anticipate challenges, mitigate risk, differentiate between a performance issue and a transition issue, and intervene effectively. The alternative is potentially losing a group with promising talents, accustomed to performing at or above expected standards, due to difficulties in acclimation. In the process, satisfaction and retention suffer, and nothing is done to bridge the gap of understanding between military and civilian worlds.

As we conclude this chapter on military transition as a matter of diversity, equity, and inclusion, take a moment to reflect on what you've learned and how you can apply it.

By completing the activities in this chapter, you've taken an important step toward creating a more inclusive environment for veterans in the civilian workplace. Awareness is the first step toward positive change.

Part 2

Essential Elements of Information

About this section:

What: Deep-dive into the Military Transition Framework™

Who: Written for the benefit of all readers

Why: To provide a structure, language, and meaning around the concept of military transition

How: Through research, anecdotes, theoretical models, and application exercises

Chapter 6

The Military Transition Framework™

"Wow, I didn't think it was going to be this different."

SAID BY COUNTLESS VETERANS IN TRANSITION

Understanding the Landscape: Why Do We Need a Framework?

THE MOST BASIC ASPECT OF THE MILITARY-TO-CIVILIAN TRANSITION IS THAT IT REPRESENTS A SIGNIFICANT LIFE CHANGE. It affects almost every aspect of life (e.g., family, community, daily routines), as opposed to the transition from one civilian job to another, which centers mostly on work and job performance. Even if a service member has prior experience managing civilians in a military context, it does not equate to working with them in a nonmilitary setting. I have consistently found that former service members who truly recognize the magnitude of this change have smoother transitions down the line.

Understanding the Magnitude of Change

Why is the magnitude of this change difficult to recognize? Because, to date, transition books and programs offered by the military prior to separation have not focused on preparing service members for civilian employment. Instead, these programs focus on preparing them for the civilian job-search process (e.g., résumé preparation or job search tips). This makes a certain amount of sense. However, as a result, veterans are often shocked by how different everything is in the civilian work environment. Many have told us that the hardest part of the military transition is grasping the concept that "you don't know what you don't know." This knowledge gap perpetuates the military-civilian divide.

A survey of former service members in the first five years of civilian employment asked how different military service was from civilian employment. The results were striking:

- 60% responded "completely different"
- 40% responded "moderately different"
- 0% reported any level of similarity

These responses highlight the significant cultural shift veterans experience when entering the civilian workforce. Let's explore why this shift is so profound.

The Root of the Issue: Military Transition Is Complex

Think back to Chapter 3 on organizational culture. Because military culture is so strong and is likely the only professional experience its members have known, other organizational cultures often seem different and, to the veteran, wrong in comparison. This cultural dissonance underscores why your ability to anticipate challenges and calibrate expectations during onboarding is so important; you'll have an easier time helping veterans acclimate to your organization if they know what to expect.

Expanding Perspectives

It reminds me of the old adage that if all you have is a hammer, everything looks like a nail. In the context of veteran transition, we can consider three possible approaches:

(1) Contort everything into the shape of a nail so you can use your hammer.

(2) Dismiss as unfit anything that can't be repurposed into a nail.

(3) Recognize that it is *you* who have the limitation, not the nail (or the hammer, for that matter), which is just being a nail.

A more apt version of this adage might be: "If all you have is a hammer, everything looks like a nail. But most things are not a nail, so your hammer will only get you so far, after which point it will utterly fail you. So you'd better get yourself some additional tools." In this scenario, the civilian line manager or HR professional is the owner of the hardware store. The more tools in stock, the better off everyone will be as a result.

It is important to note that any new employee coming from another strong organizational culture will need some help updating their toolbox.

Navigating the Journey: How to Use the Military Transition Framework™ (MTF)

Given the complexity of this transition, a structured approach can be beneficial. This is where the Military Transition Framework™ comes in. After many years of working with veterans in civilian organizations, I began to observe consistent patterns. I saw three distinct stages, which I labeled detaching, regrouping, and integrating. Individuals who transitioned smoothly into civilian success seemed to progress through the stages fairly quickly. Individuals who struggled with the transition—letting go of the military way of working and adopting the civilian way of working—seemed to get stuck in one or both of the first two stages.

After extensive research and testing, I developed a model to illustrate the process, now known as the Military Transition Framework™ or MTF. (See below.) Similar to Bridges's model of life transitions discussed in Chapter 1, the MTF has three stages. However, in Bridges's description, each stage must be completed before one can move on to the next stage, whereas the MTF is fluid. Why? because there are no clear boundaries between stages; the stages occur organically, reflecting the complexity of military transition.

The Three Stages of the MTF:

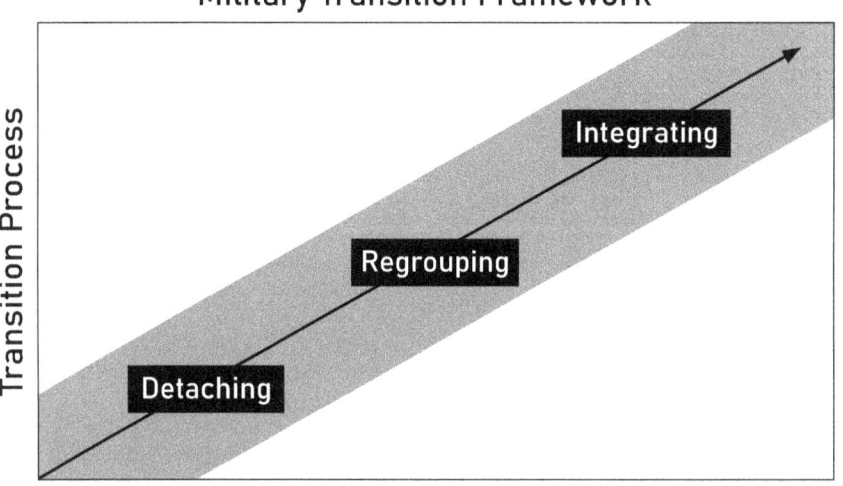

Military Transition Framework™

(1) Detaching: This stage is internally focused and involves a significant shift in identity for a veteran to succeed in civilian employment. Detaching is characterized by a mix of feelings, thoughts, and behavior changes as the veteran mentally and emotionally steps away from the military lifestyle.

(2) Regrouping: Focused on external interactions, regrouping involves interacting with people and work in a civilian context. This stage can be lengthy, as it encompasses extensive learning about civilian work culture, beyond the new-hire orientation. Regrouping is about applying the skills, knowledge, and abilities acquired in the military to effectively operate in a civilian context.

Note: Military transition assistance programs typically do not teach service members to detach or regroup. As an employer, it's crucial for HR or line managers to support veterans through this stage to reduce errors, accelerate learning, and position them for success.

(3) Integrating: This final stage signifies the successful culmination of the transition journey, both internally for the individual and externally in their behavior. Veterans achieve integration when they smoothly adapt to new ways of doing things and effectively apply their military skills in ways that add value to the civilian organization, while also experiencing a sense of satisfaction and belonging.

While the movement between stages is fluid, each stage has clear differentiators. Detaching is an *internal process* related to attitudes, feelings, beliefs, habits, and interpretations. It occurs in private and can inform behavior. An example from my days as a consultant. If I had unresolved hard feelings about how I left my last project, I may bring that baggage into the next project and behave in ways that are off-putting to my colleagues, such as being defensive or withdrawn.

Regrouping, on the other hand, is an *external process* based in behavior that can be observed by others. To use my previous example, by working through my hard feelings about a recent project, I will approach the new project unburdened and ready to learn and contribute. The way I show up for my colleagues will be very different than in the previous example. Regrouping can be identified by increasing levels of receptivity and experimentation with the organization's way of doing things.

Detaching and Regrouping almost always overlap as the veteran gradually adapts to the new ways of doing and being. For example, a new job may not come with training right away, so the veteran will naturally perform tasks as they would have in the military, unaware of new ways of approaching the work. If this veteran has completed Detaching, they likely expect and welcome guidance on how to accomplish tasks. If the veteran has not completed Detaching, they may be less open to new approaches to the work.

In most cases where I am brought into a company to coach veterans, it is because they are stuck in the Detaching stage and need coaching to progress into Regrouping. Coaching has been proven many times over to be the best way of accelerating this learning process.

In the Military Transition Framework, movement from one stage to another occurs over time. The length of time spent in each stage is different for every veteran. That said, working through *At Ease* will accelerate the transition.

Now that we've outlined the stages, let's consider how employers can support veterans through each phase.

Moving Forward: Action Steps for Success

With the MTF in mind, here are some key strategies for employers to effectively support veterans through their transition:

1. Recognize the transition stage: Understand that you don't know where in the transition process any given new hire will be when they join your organization.

2. Provide comprehensive onboarding: Debunk assumptions early on in the cultural assimilation process.

3. Offer mentoring and coaching: Train managers and HR professionals in skills associated with mentoring and coaching as necessary feedback mechanisms.

4. Be patient and understanding: Avoid assuming that military hires are willfully resisting change. Give the benefit of the doubt when there's a question of intention.

5. Clarify expectations: Clearly define the expectations of your particular workplace.

6. Explain the "why": Provide rationale—the "why"—of the organization's way of doing things, and share what success looks like in your organization.

Closing Thoughts

Initially, service members may not be attuned to how people are responding to them, even in a nuanced way, and may not see that anything needs to change. Specifically, the military can be more straightforward. You'll want to avoid the assumption that such military hires are willfully resisting change. Assume the opposite: give the benefit of the doubt when there is a question regarding intention, because nine times out of ten, the people involved are completely unaware of their missteps. Clarify the expectations of *your* particular workplace. In addition, if you can define the intent—the "why"—of success and what it looks like even in a chaotic and rapidly changing environment, it will enable the individual new hire to take initiative, feel ownership, and provide feedback and suggestions for best practices. This is practical guidance for use with any and all new hires, but especially with those coming to you from the military.

Want to know where you are in the military transition process? Veterans and service members interested in taking the Military Transition Framework Assessment can do so at no cost. See the *Resources page* at the back of the book.

Civilian managers and HR professionals benefit from training in skills associated with mentoring and coaching as necessary feedback mechanisms. *See Resources page at the end of the book.*

As we've seen, the military-to-civilian transition is a complex process that requires understanding and support from both veterans and their new employers. In the following chapters, we'll explore each stage of the Military Transition Framework™ in greater detail, providing specific strategies to support the success and retention of your military hires.

Chapter 7

Detaching

"My whole life had been defined by the military. [Transition is] a whole change process, and I think a lot of people just take off the uniform on Friday and go back to work on Monday for a government job or contractor and they never really take the time to go through that process. To be open to the change and understand that you may have been hired because of what you know from the military, is not what's going to keep you successful."

—OFFICER, U.S. ARMY[25]

Understanding the Landscape: What Is the Detaching Stage of the MTF?

IN THE CONTEXT OF MILITARY TRANSITION, I DEFINE "DETACH" AS A VERB, meaning to mentally step away from the defined lifestyle of the military. Detaching is an internal process characterized by a mix of feelings, thoughts, and behavior changes.

It is easiest to recognize detaching by its absence. There is a commonly used expression to describe the individual who has not detached from the military; it is said that they need to "take off the uniform." Even though this is a metaphor, it can also be interpreted literally in terms of the actual physical uniform. The service member has traded a long-worn uniform for civilian garb. He or she is the same person as before, but military accomplishments and hard-earned status are suddenly invisible without the uniform.

> "When you transition into the civilian world, you do have to prove yourself all over again. You're very much an unknown commodity to the civilian world. They know—certainly the employers recognize that you did something—you did well in the military, you did good things; but you're just one of the workforce now and that loss of prestige, I think, is hard for some officers to deal with after literally spending an entire lifetime's career achieving and then enjoying it."
>
> —OFFICER, USAF[26]

Individuals who are still in uniform, so to speak, after their formal separation from the military have some consistent behaviors. For example, they may cope with the ambiguity of a personnel policy by imposing structure and limits on things that shouldn't be structured or limited, and unwittingly damage employee morale. Or they may insist on doing things the military way even if it creates stress for themselves and others. It is not unusual to hear an overuse of openers such as, "When I was in the military" or "That's not how it's done on my watch," which demonstrate a resistance to other, nonmilitary ways of doing things.

> "A trap that military guys can fall into is to say, 'I used to be somebody, and let me tell you all the cool things I did.' So there's a certain need to win acceptance because people just look right past you. They don't even know you used to be somebody. You're just some guy. So that can fire up an urge to overtell about your expe-

rience. What I found useful was the less I said about the Marine Corps, the better off I was. And the best way I found to refer to previous experience was to simply say, 'In a previous life I once had this experience that I did this,' and I always described it functionally."

—OFFICER, USMC[27]

The Root of the Issue: Why the Detaching Stage of the MTF Is Difficult

The number one goal of Detaching is to constructively separate from the previous identity as a military service member, to "take off the uniform." This is directly related to success as a civilian professional because it is a necessary precursor to integrating. "Taking off the uniform" is not only an essential part of the transition process, but it is often the most difficult. For the duration of one's military career, the uniform was a clear and undeniable symbol of identity. By design, the uniform signaled to others how to address one another and kept a vast number of personnel organized and focused on the military's mission. The most common feeling experienced to some degree, especially by those with ten or more years of service, is a sense of loss. This is a natural response to the transition that seems to linger with time if left unaddressed.

You may be wondering how this can be the case given that career military personnel are used to integrating into new cultures and duty stations every few years. In fact, many service members consider this part of the joy of service. They pride themselves on their ability to drop into a new environment and be immediately effective. Many describe a change of duty station as both seamless—thanks to the military infrastructure—and exciting. So in essence, all else being equal, it's a relatively smooth transition. Understandably, many long-term service members expect the transition to civilian employment to be like a change of duty station, but it's not. Far from it. In civilian organizations, all else is *not* equal. Not even close. It's unlike any previous career move they have made.

Civilian organizations generally can't lay claim to employee identity because their employees come and go every day, and think of their jobs as just one aspect of life. They don't live on a base where they work, where their kids go to school, where they work with their neighbors. Many service members have been living in a family-oriented community that's connected by a set of shared values and protocols of behavior, in which home life and work life are closely aligned and mutually supportive.

> "In the military, even those who only sign up for three or four years kind of throw themselves into it. I had never encountered people who worked to live, not lived to work. It was a bit of a shockaroo to me that a person could actually make a life choice that 'I'm going to make a paycheck to support the thing that matters to me … which is not here.'"
>
> —OFFICER, USMC[28]

Detaching is a very personal process of defining self differently, and it is important to know and accept it as a process … NOT a deliverable.

Navigating the Journey: How to Put Down Your DRUMS

The military is notorious for its use of acronyms, so in that spirit I coined the acronym DRUMS to illustrate the challenge of Detaching. It stands for Default Reaction: Use Military Style. Under stress or uncertainty, most of us fall back on what we're accustomed to—our comfort zone. For a service member, this "default" reaction will be to use what worked in the military, also known as "command and control." However, this approach can be problematic in civilian workplaces.

By definition, DRUMS can overpower other perspectives and approaches. In civilian settings, DRUMS may come across as overly aggressive, directive, or inflexible. This can damage work relationships, create barriers between people, and hinder collaboration and learning.

> "I worked with a career officer who had a hard time adapting to civilian culture. When he would meet resistance, his behavior pattern would revert to even more of the military behavior that allowed him to succeed there which, of course, further exacerbated the situation. He developed a reputation as someone who wasn't able to think creatively, who viewed life and the business world as checklist-oriented, and someone who would growl at you. This created problems in his civilian peer group and with his staff."
>
> —OFFICER, USAF[29]

To successfully integrate into civilian work culture, veterans must learn to tone down their DRUMS. This involves acknowledging that there are multiple valid approaches to accomplishing tasks, not just the military way. It's crucial for new-hire veterans to understand early on that different methods are not only acceptable but often preferred in civilian environments. Using a strict military approach may actually hinder their success and create unnecessary challenges.

Veterans

To help veterans recognize and address their DRUMS, we've developed a two-part activity. This exercise aims to raise awareness about how military-style behaviors might impact others in civilian workplaces and provide strategies for adapting more effectively. The first part involves self-reflection, while the second part encourages seeking feedback from civilian colleagues.[30]

Practical Application for Veterans

Activity—Putting Down the DRUMS, Part 1

DRUMS is our acronym for "Default Reaction: Use Military Style." It is natural to rely upon habitual or automatic responses, especially during times of stress. However, the military style of interacting with others is often viewed as off-putting in a civilian work environment. Therefore, you will need to be observant of the impact you have on others, and modify as indicated.

Purpose: To raise your awareness of the impact you have on others.

Directions: You may want to get help on this activity from a close friend or family member, as it seeks to reveal what you don't know about how you come across.

1. Reflect on an interaction in which something you did or said was met with a negative or confused reaction from a civilian.
2. Use the prompts below to describe what occurred

Situation: _____

_____

_____

_____

Your words and/or actions: _____

_____

_____

_____

_____

*Your underlying intention:*_____

_____

_____

_____

*The other person's reaction:*_____

_____

_____

_____

Possible interpretations of their reaction:

1 _____ .

_____

2 _____ .

_____

3 _____ .

_____

4 _____ .

_____

*Consider all you might learn about your impact on others by exploring this further with the individual in question. For example, you might ask for a follow-up to clarify, and then share your observation of what happened **along with your intention** and, in a spirit of interest and curiosity, **ask about their reaction**. Think back to the activities you completed earlier about assumptions. You may well find that by sharing your intention and understanding the other's reaction, you build a bridge to a more positive working relationship.*

Activity—Putting Down the DRUMS, Part 2

There's nothing like honest feedback from a trusted source to shake up our self-perceptions. Regardless of how self-aware we may be, there are times when we are surprised by another person's response to us. If the goal of communication is to have our message understood as intended, we want to be on top of how we are sending those messages.

Purpose: To increase awareness of how you come across to others so you can align your intentions with your actual impact.

Directions:

1. Identify two or three civilians with whom you have a trusting relationship, and ask them to give you the gift of honest feedback. Consider using the following prompts:

    a. What could get me into trouble with civilians who don't know me?

    b. What habits or characteristics would endear me to them?

    c. What were your first impressions of me?

    d. How would you describe my communication style?

    e. Imagine me working in a civilian environment: What advice would you give me?

2. Make note of what you learn so you can identify opportunities and strategies for communicating so that your intention—not just your words—gets across.

By completing both parts of this activity, veterans can gain valuable insights into how their military-influenced behaviors may impact their civilian colleagues. This awareness is the first step in learning to adjust their approach for greater success in their new work environment.

Practical Application for Employers: Coaching Conversations Can Help

The most powerful thing you can do to support veterans through Detaching is to practice active listening. Why? Because it allows the veteran to verbally process their experience in a nonjudging context. Hearing oneself speak is helpful in itself, and hearing our words summarized and spoken back to us by a good listener can advance our thinking. Active listening helps to normalize the transition experience for the veteran, which is also supportive. A good listener provides space for reflection and problem solving.

As a professional leadership coach, I know firsthand the powerful impact of listening and validating the experience of a transitioning veteran. Listening without judgment, listening to learn and understand, is a gift to the speaker and something many have never experienced. The following is an example of what I would call a "coaching conversation," but which can be initiated by you or anyone who wants to help veterans transition. One does not need to be a professional coach to do a good job of listening and asking purposeful questions.

Coaching Conversation: Transition Process

Coach: Charlie, you're wrapping up your first week with us. How's it going?

Charlie: Oh, it's a whirlwind, but very positive. I can't wait to dig in and contribute.

Coach: I know it can be frustrating to figure out how to do your job in a new environment.

Charlie: Yes, I keep calling my manager "Sir," and he keeps correcting me!

Coach: What has it been like for you, leaving military service?

Charlie: Oh, every day is an adventure—I never know what's coming. It seems I've lost all my familiar daily routines. Kind of disorienting!

Coach: Routines are comforting! What routines would you like to integrate into your civilian life?

Charlie: I think getting home in time to have dinner with my family would be helpful for all of us—we are all acclimating to the fluctuating work schedule and haven't crossed paths too much this week.

Coach: That does sound important. Is there anything I can do to help make that happen?

Charlie: Well, I guess it would be good to know if leaving at 5:00 p.m. is acceptable or frowned upon. ... I notice a lot of cars in the office parking lot long after dark!

Coach: I know what you mean, and I think each person has to make his or her own choices about that kind of thing. It's something you may want to ask your manager, who may have specific expectations about work hours.

Coach: What has surprised you the most about leaving military service?

Charlie: Definitely the loss of camaraderie. I'm used to having my friends around me when I work, seeing neighbors at the commissary, going to events at my kids' school on base. Now everything feels kind of disconnected.

Coach: That sounds like a big adjustment. How are you coping with it?

Charlie: Initially, it was kind of a letdown… I was excited about leaving the military and starting my new life, but then it felt like the rug was pulled out from under me. At least when I changed jobs and duty stations in the military, it was still the military and a lot remained the same from place to place. Things just got taken care of for you. Now, nothing gets done unless I do it myself!

Coach: I imagine that could be overwhelming. I know from working with other veterans over the years that it all takes time to get used to, and pacing yourself can help a lot. I know someone in the finance department who left service about a year ago and faced some of the same challenges you're describing. I'd like to introduce you to each other so you can benefit from what he learned along the way. Would you be interested in that?

Charlie: Yes! That would be great! It is always quicker to learn from someone else's mistakes than to make them all yourself!

Moving Forward: Action Steps for Success

While many service members eagerly anticipate civilian life, the transition can be more challenging for those with longer military careers. The length of service often correlates with the depth of military culture ingrained in an individual, making the shift to civilian life more complex. Service members who approach civilian employment with a positive and enthusiastic posture tend to move quickly through the detaching stage because they aren't resisting change. These individuals often come across as being:

- Open to whatever the world may present them with
- Humble about the fact that they are newbies when it comes to being civilians

- Successful earlier in their civilian careers because they can adapt quickly
- Receptive to civilian culture and operations

Accelerating Progress

For veterans, the most effective way to accelerate your progress is to keep doing what you're doing now: applying yourself to the content and activities in *At Ease*. Enroll in our Accelerated Military Transition Course or work with an AMTC certified coach.

For employers, to accelerate veterans' progress through the framework, there are many ways of going about it. For example,

- Integrating our content into new-hire orientation for veterans
- Providing veteran new hires with *At Ease* upon employment
- Providing our Accelerated Military Transition Course (AMTC) to new hires and their managers
- Offering AMTC coaching to individuals or groups in your organization
- Engaging your organization's military/veteran ERG in some or all of the above

Practical Applications for Veterans:

Accelerating the Detaching Stage, Part 1

Now that we've explored the concept of Detaching and identified key techniques to support this process, let's engage in an activity that will help you apply these insights to your own transition journey. This exercise focuses on seven characteristics or best practices that have been proven to contribute to a smooth transition from military to civilian life.

Purpose: To incorporate mindsets and behaviors associated with a smooth military transition

Directions:

1. Review the characteristics below, which research has found to correlate with a smooth military transition:

    A. Observing external cues about your impact on others

    B. Thinking forward, not backward

    C. Translating directives into requests

    D. Acknowledging the magnitude of change related to military transition

    E. Accepting the ambiguity of starting something new (in this case, you are starting to not be in the military)

    F. Taking time to explore and discover who you are without the uniform

    G. Welcoming new ways of operating, with an open mind

2. Pick the two that are most likely to pose a challenge for you, and explain why:

_____

_____

_____

_____

_____

_____

_____

3. How can/will you begin to address these challenges so they don't become a barrier to your success as a civilian?

_____

_____

_____

By reflecting on these characteristics and developing strategies to address potential challenges, you'll be better equipped to navigate the detaching process and set yourself up for success in your civilian career. Remember, the goal is not to abandon your military experience, but to adapt and apply your skills in ways that are effective in your new civilian environment.

Veterans: To further solidify the concepts we've explored in this chapter and to help you apply them to your own experience, complete the reflective activity below. It will help you personalize the Detaching process and prepare you for the next phase: Regrouping.

Accelerating the Detaching Stage, Part 2

Purpose: To personalize the concepts described in this chapter to your own transition experience and to learn as much as you can from Detaching to facilitate moving into Regrouping.

Directions: Reflect on and respond to the following questions:

1. What resonates with me about Detaching? What do I relate to?

2. Based on my new awareness of Detaching, what do I want to remain aware of in order to avoid mistakes in this phase?

Remember, Detaching is a personal journey, and everyone's experience will be unique. Be patient with yourself as you navigate this process, and don't hesitate to seek support when you need it. Your experiences in the military have equipped you with valuable skills and perspectives—the key is learning how to adapt and apply them effectively in your new civilian environment.

Closing Thoughts

Resistance to new approaches and attachment to military approaches is a common indicator that an individual is still working through the Detaching stage. Ideally, the individual is well into the Detaching process before starting a new job, but "ideal" is the operative word here, as it rarely happens that way. The important thing is that you as a transitioning veteran attend to the task of Detaching even if it means doing so after work hours, by working through *At Ease* and the other books recommended herein. It will allow you to mentally "take off the uniform" and consider who you might be without it. This process of reflection allows you to make thoughtful choices about employment rather than jumping at the first opportunity that comes your way. This in turn increases the likelihood of a good fit. Detaching can be a period of great personal growth.

Chapter 8

Regrouping

Understanding the Landscape: What Is the Regrouping Stage of the MTF?

"I was given a task as soon as I started working and I was expected to complete it with only a minimal amount of knowledge of how. ... So I had to ask a lot of questions and depend on other personnel to help me accomplish the task rather than be able to find a reference or manual to read and direct me. That made me feel kind of inadequate even though I had completed twenty-four years in the Marine Corps and I was, at one time, the go-to person on getting things done. I felt very small. In the Marine Corps you have a Directive on almost every subject, so that was a little difficult to get used to."

—ENLISTED SERVICE MEMBER, USMC[31]

THE SECOND STAGE IN THE MILITARY TRANSITION FRAMEWORK IS REGROUPING. Moving into this stage from Detaching is a gradual process. The best clue that a veteran is approaching or entering the Regrouping stage is their lack of resistance to new ideas and ways of working. There is less referencing the past and more focus on the present and future. For example, referencing the past may sound like, "Back when I was in the military, we did it this way." Focusing on the present and future may sound like, "In my new job, we have a great approach to dealing with client complaints," or "I look forward to learning from other teams who have faced this challenge."

Unlike Detaching, which is an internal identity-related process, Regrouping is an external behavior-related process in which the veteran is continually confronted with new ways of doing things and approaches that conflict with military practice. Key aspects of this stage of transition are a steep learning curve, reduced resistance to change, increasing capacity to receive and respond nondefensively to feedback, and, ultimately, adoption of ways of working and interacting that align with the organization's culture.

The Root of the Issue: Why the Regrouping Stage of the MTF Is Difficult

Regrouping does not necessarily begin after detaching has been completed. The two stages are not dependent upon each other that way. Regrouping begins when the service member is first faced with the unfamiliar world of civilian employment. This may be during the job-search process when they start to experience how different a civilian organization is from the military in terms of language, priorities, values, and organizational cultures. Regrouping comes into full force as new hires engage with their new employer.

As one might expect, adopting new ways of thinking, doing, and being is more easily done when one is not resisting change.

Perhaps the biggest challenge of Regrouping is trying to do it while fully immersed in the Detaching process. Regrouping can be fraught with frustration, interpersonal missteps, unnecessary anxiety, and resistance to the new reality. This is challenging to the individual as well as to those at the receiving end. Those who might genuinely try to help the service member succeed find it frustrating to stand by and watch the individual get in his or her own way time and time again until they either quit or experience a significant mental shift.

Veterans themselves say it best, so let's look at Regrouping through the eyes of some veterans kind enough to share what it was like for them:

"Most of the disciplines learned in the military aren't perceived the same in the civilian world, so I had to adapt. Conforming to the civilian's version of what's accepted, preferred and frowned upon was frustrating because it caused me to be 'tripped up,' although it was unintentional."

—ENLISTED SERVICE MEMBER, US COAST GUARD[32]

"[The civilian world] seemed confusing and chaotic for me coming out of the service, while things were more organized and defined in the military. In the service I felt I had people willing to instruct me and it was more direct on the success and failure side. 'Do these tasks and you will be successful.' In civilian life it is, 'You do these tasks and if we like your style or personality, you will be successful.'"

—ENLISTED SERVICE MEMBER, US NAVY[33]

In Part 1, we discussed the many cultural differences that can make military transition challenging. Those all come to life in Regrouping. For example, learning about communication and decision-making styles, the role of organizational mission, and what it means to lead a voluntary workforce—this is the learning of the Regrouping stage.

"In the military, particularly once you gain rank, people assume that you're kind of right. And so, even though you want to get everybody's perspective, people put more stock and value in whatever you say and generally go in that direction. I found on the civilian side, you get a lot more done if you get people collaborating, get everybody's input, and go forward from there. It may not be the right solution. I guess it's more important to make some progress for all concerned than it is to be right. My experience working with civilians says it's more important to get everybody to buy into a solution even though it might not be your version of the right solution. You'll make much more progress by getting everybody involved."

—OFFICER, US ARMY[34]

At its essence, the challenge of Regrouping is finding the right balance of focus on task (mission) and focus on relationship. To master civilian culture, it is imperative to understand the nature of tasks and relationships because the two exist in parallel. What do I mean by this? In the military, when a direct order is given, it is carried out as part of the standard operating procedure. Because the civilian mission is different, its workplace is less structured and *relationships replace protocol as the way to get things done.* In civilian life, no one is compelled to follow orders to the letter or on a specific time frame. Direct reports should and generally do care about performing well against the boss's standards, but what about the boss's peers and other colleagues? They have their own priorities. So it is easier and quicker to get things done if the person you are requesting help from knows and feels favorably toward you.

"Sometimes you've got to look at your long-term relationships and not just being so mission-focused. That was a big light bulb for me, and so I do act differently within my organization and actually think a little bit differently because of that. ... It definitely has gotten better. My colleagues are more receptive to me personally because of this attitude change in how I approach and listen to people. It also has helped me to get some perspective that I normally would have just discounted. Now that my perspective is much wider, I'm going to listen to everybody's opinions."

—OFFICER, USAF[35]

A key difference between military and civilian operating styles relates to communication. We spoke earlier about how the military's culture and operations are designed to support its mission. As such, both the written and spoken communication style is clear, direct, and informational. Some civilians might say "terse." It is preferable to convey a message in as few words as possible than to search for the most sensitive or eloquent way of saying it. In the military, expedience is valued over tone. Everybody shares the same context.

Because the civilian workplace is often concerned with profit, both the purpose and style of communication are different. Communicating to build rapport, set a tone, influence opinion, close a sale, calm a client, or convey emotion require a softer touch than you may be used to.

How something is said often matters as much if not more than what is actually said. In fact, if the way something is communicated is too succinct, the message may be lost altogether. If your tone is harsh, aggressive, or overly direct, the audience (of any size) will focus on why you're speaking to them in that way rather than focusing on what you are actually saying. A good rule of thumb is to remember the importance of building rapport, which means slowing down and balancing clarity with approachability.

This shift in perspective highlights a crucial aspect of civilian workplace dynamics. In any given interaction, regardless of urgency, there is room to promote or damage the connection with others. As we all know, trust takes a long time to build and even longer to rebuild if lost.

Practical Application: Email Communication

To illustrate the challenges of Regrouping, let's examine a real-life email exchange between Al, a civilian peer, and Tom, a former Army Lt. Colonel. This exchange highlights common communication pitfalls veterans may encounter during their transition:

E-Mail Exchange

From: Al (civilian peer)
Date/Time: Sept. 8th, 11:00 am
To: Tom (former Army Lt. Col.)
Subject: Presentation slides

Good morning Tom: Some of my staff over here in the Systems team attended yesterday's symposium and heard your presentation. I'd like to take you up on the offer to get the slides in soft copy, since the topic relates to the work we're doing. The slides will be a good resource for the team going forward.
Thanks and I look forward to hearing from you.
Al

From: Tom
Date/Time: Sept. 8th, 11:05 am
To: Al
Subject: Re: Presentation slides

Give me some times you're available
r/
Tom

2:30 pm.: Al returns to his desk after several meetings, and begins reading through the fifteen email messages awaiting him. He comes to Tom's response and has no clue what it means. He asks himself, "What does my availability have to do with sending the slides over email?" Al looks back at his sent message to remind himself of the context. Still puzzled, he sends this reply:

From: Al
Date/Time: Sept. 8th, 2:35 pm
To: Tom
Subject: RE: Presentation slides

Tom, are you asking what time I'd be available to pick them up? I was hoping you could just email the document.
Thanks, Al
p.s. What is "r/"?

From: Tom
Date/Time: Sept 8th, 2:37 pm
Subject: Re: Presentation slides

Assuming you want to go over the presentation.

Al reads this and thinks, "What's with the cryptic answers? Could this guy make it any harder to get this done? Forget it! I don't have time to go back and forth on this." Al walks away from the exchange with a feeling of exasperation and annoyance with Tom.

After reviewing this exchange, it's clear that miscommunication can easily occur between veterans and their civilian colleagues. To better understand and address these issues, consider the following questions:

Putting It All Together

Monday Morning Quarterback

What went awry in the email exchange between Al and Tom? As an objective third party, how would you explain it?

How would you advise Al to enable a more productive exchange with Tom in the future?

How would you advise Tom to enable a more productive exchange with Al in the future?

What are some things you could say or do to prevent this initial disconnect from occurring between veterans and civilians in the future?

The email exchange and subsequent questions demonstrate how different communication styles can lead to misunderstandings. Let's explore how successful Regrouping manifests in behavioral changes:

Before and After Regrouping

Before Regrouping	*After Regrouping*
1. "Oh, I've done this before. The best way to do it is this way…"	1. "I've done something like this in another context and I wonder if it would work here."
2. "I keep telling them exactly what's going to happen if they do it that way, but no one wants to hear it."	2. "The team needs to feel a sense of ownership for this to work, so we're exploring the options together for now."
3. "I don't know why they left me out of the loop on this, since it is why they hired me."	3. "This looks like an oversight. I'll offer my insight and see if they take me up on it."
4. "I'm just waiting for one of my buddies to get me into his company."	4. "At first I thought this place was nuts, but it didn't take long to see that I was the one that needed to adjust. Glad I realized it when I did."

Navigating the Journey: How to Accelerate the Regrouping Stage of the MTF

As we can see, successful Regrouping involves significant shifts in mindset and behavior. Veterans who have successfully navigated the Regrouping stage often display the following characteristics:

- Have a healthy respect for the unknown and err on the side of caution vs. assumption.
- Feel energized by their own new ideas and those of others, including staff.
- Welcome new experiences and an alternative way of doing things.
- Are flexible in interpreting rules.
- Fully bring their skill and experience to bear, while remaining humble about what they do not know or understand.
- Are willing to roll up their sleeves and be "doers" when necessary.
- Continually practice the skills of listening, observing, and inquiring to gain valuable information, and adopt an interpersonal style different from that of the military.

Feedback

"Feedback was faster and more clear (direct) in the military than in civilian life, leading to more stress after leaving the military. … Civilian managers should be told that those of us recently discharged will be fine with direct, clear feedback. We are less likely to get hurt feelings over it since constant improvement is a military theme we understand."—Navy Petty Officer (E-5)

Over the last twenty years, I've consulted to organizations large and small, and "lack of sufficient feedback" is an abiding theme and the code no one can seem to crack; the issue just will not go away. I see the same trends in employee surveys that I did in the '90s; literally. Here are a few:

- Employees at all organizational levels rate feedback in the top three priorities
- Employees report that they don't get enough feedback

- Supervisors and managers report that they do provide feedback

See the gap? My observations are backed up by none other than the Gallup organization, which adds an important link: feedback leads to engagement; engagement leads to retention. Here's what Gallup said in its "Seven Workplace Insights" from 2020:

- Employee engagement is a strong predictor of performance during tough times
- Frequent feedback is the primary lever of engagement among remote workers
- Even those who receive negative feedback wish they received more feedback[36]

The number of workshops and slides designed to respond to this ongoing call for feedback is staggering. And the evidence is piling up to support feedback as a critical component of employee engagement and retention. Yet the issue persists. Consider this:

Machines learn from feedback constantly provided by users. It's not a "thing." There isn't a discrete event in the user experience called "giving the machine feedback so it learns." It is happening just by virtue of a user using and a machine running. It is standard operating procedure. Make no mistake: preparation is needed. The machine must be configured to learn, and users must be taught to operate the machine. But is performance feedback so different? Why is it so hard for organizations to ingrain it as standard operating procedure?

In my humble opinion, the answer lies in something management guru Peter Drucker said many years ago:

"The most serious mistakes are not being made as a result of wrong answers.

The truly dangerous thing is asking the wrong questions."

Companies are asking the wrong question. Instead of asking, "How can we increase the amount and quality of feedback?" they should be asking, "How can we create an intentional culture in which feedback is not a discrete event but, rather, the standard operating procedure—the natural flow of conversation through-out the day?" Then, rather than producing ever more how-to-do-it trainings and campaigns, they could solve for the root cause: how-to-be-it; how to be a place where feedback is SOP.

"Feedback is not a thing. It is a way."

That's brilliant! Who said that? I did. Just now. You can quote me on it. Consider this reframe: instead of viewing giving and receiv-ing feedback as skills to be acquired for use at periodic intervals over a period of performance, view them as the primary channel through which business is conducted from moment to moment. Kind of like the AI example. By doing this, we may finally be able to crack the code on organizational feedback and, in so doing, build a new, bigger/badder neural pathway when it comes to human performance in the workplace.

This insight into the importance of feedback underscores the need for a holistic approach to supporting veterans' transitions.

To help you apply the concepts we've discussed and reflect on your own Regrouping process, let's engage in an activity designed to synthesize your learning and apply it to your life. This exercise will encourage you to think critically about your transition and identify areas for growth and improvement.

Moving Forward: Action Steps for Success

Activity: Reflect on Regrouping

Purpose: To apply the concept of Regrouping to yourself and your military transition

Directions: Reflect and respond to the following questions:

1. My current understanding of Regrouping: _____

_____

_____

_____

_____

_____

_____

_____

2. I identify with these aspects of Regrouping: _____

_____

_____

_____

_____

_____

_____

3. Based on what I'm learning about myself and Regrouping, I want to do and/or remain aware of the following, so as to avoid missteps:

_____

_____

_____

By completing this activity, you'll gain deeper insights into your own Regrouping process and develop strategies to navigate the challenges of transitioning to civilian work life more effectively. Remember, successful Regrouping is a journey that requires patience, self-awareness, and a willingness to adapt and learn.

Closing Thoughts

Successful Regrouping means an individual has toned down the DRUMS enough to hear and see what's happening outside of themself and modify behavior based on external clues about the new environment. This adaptation is critical for veterans to thrive in civilian workplaces. It is a continual process, and I've found mindset makes all the difference. Specifically, get okay with feeling like a beginner again. It takes humility and curiosity. Humor helps a lot. Remember, your military transition may feel uncomfortable, but it doesn't have to define you. You are still the skilled and accomplished person you were in the military. AND you are in the process of becoming just as skilled and accomplished in a totally new context.

Chapter 9

Integrating

Understanding the Landscape: What Is the Integrating Stage of the MTF?

INTEGRATING IS THE THIRD AND FINAL STAGE IN THE MILITARY TRANSITION FRAMEWORK™. It is the destination of the military transition journey. You will know former service members have completed detaching and regrouping and entered integrating when you see them working *with* the flow (rather than against the flow), smoothly adapting to new ways of doing things. This is most evident when a veteran new hire joins the organization and you think to yourself, "Oh yeah, I remember making that mistake when I got here!" or "Oh, yes, I remember so-and-so making that mistake when he was new. He would never do that now."

Signposts of Integrating

I have seen integration demonstrated in myriad ways, sometimes simply by the absence of issues and challenges. Other things to look for include:

- More expansive thinking, free of resistance to nonmilitary interpretations
- Less defensiveness about what isn't known or understood
- Capacity to use humor to lighten uncomfortable moments
- Ability to transfer and translate previous experience into valuable assets
- Ability to blend new ways of operating with those that made them successful before
- Ability to establish trust and credibility by embracing the methods of others
- Consistent performance at a high level and stretching professionally
- Genuine enjoyment of the job, colleagues, and new civilian self
- Openness to/excitement about the possibility of a long-term role in the organization

Comments I've heard from veterans who are fully integrated into their civilian environments include things like "I'm really enjoying the freedom I now have to try different approaches. If I have an idea that sounds interesting, I usually get the green light to give it a try. Then we assess afterwards to see how it worked." Or "My first few months out were tough because it was like learning a new language. But I'm getting it now and I feel like I am finally making a contribution." Or "Things aren't always written down in terms of rules of engagement. There have been some awkward learning opportunities, but we just laugh about them afterwards."

Navigating the Journey: How to Lean Into the Integrating Stage

Manage Your Career

Integrating doesn't mean the veteran stops learning or never makes another mistake. It means they have let go of norms from the military and opened their mind to another way of doing and being. Even when things go wrong, they now have them in perspective and can address them constructively. It is a mindset that says they have taken off the uniform.

In many organizations, integration looks like readiness for promotion or added responsibility. It may not be possible to put a finger on what has shifted in the veteran, but it is enough simply to observe that they now "get it" about working effectively in the environment. There is no timeline for when an individual reaches integration because it is the culmination of internal and external transition, both highly personal processes.

While integration is often viewed by observers as readiness for what's next, it is also the point where a former service member begins to think about career management. This should not be confused with the job-hopping that can occur during detaching or regrouping, which is based on dissatisfaction with current employment; rather, career management in the integration stage is about owning one's career and making thoughtful decisions about how to build on success. After all, it is difficult to contemplate success at the next level while one is struggling to be successful at the current level. When the energy spent in the struggle can be directed toward career planning, integration has most likely occurred. More on career development in Chapter 12.

Develop Others

The spirit of service runs deep in service members, and they love to help more than any other group with which I've worked. If they can smooth the transition of fellow veterans entering the civilian workforce, they are often eager to do so. Integration is the best time to engage them as mentors or learning buddies for military new hires. Having completed the detaching and regrouping stages of the transition, these employees have the wisdom of experience and the scratches (but not scars) to go with it, and they have a great success story to tell your new hires. Invite them to help out one-to-one or with groups of new hires.

There is another key role integrated veterans can play in your organization in support of their fellows coming in: the role of subject matter expert when it comes to successful military-to-civilian transition. Your program to hire and retain veterans will be well served by the insight and experience of those who have successfully integrated into your organization.

As you progress in your integration journey, you may find yourself in a leadership position within your civilian organization. This transition from military to civilian leadership requires a shift in communication style and expectations. The following activity is designed to help you clearly communicate your leadership style and expectations to your civilian team.

Leading Teams

Research shows that strong leaders tend to demonstrate high levels of emotional intelligence (EQ). EQ is the capacity to effectively deal with emotions (yours and others') in stressful situations. This requires leaders to have a high degree of self-awareness about their stress triggers and reactions, and the ability to monitor themselves during stress. Leaders with emotional intelligence can identify a range of emotions in themselves and in others, and effectively guide individuals and teams through challenging situations in a manner that promotes positive outcomes and relationships.

At some point in your military career, you most likely received feedback on your personality style. Perhaps you received a profile of your management or leadership tendencies. The U.S. military uses style assessments (e.g., MBTI) to help leaders understand themselves better and build on the strengths of teams. In your civilian career, it can be helpful to share your insights with the teams you lead so they can get to know and understand you as you are getting to know and understand them.

Practical Application for Veterans

Activity: Help Your Team Get to Know You

Purpose:

To gain personal insight; to communicate with staff in explicit terms your expectations and style preferences, so everyone is off to a good start under your leadership

Directions:

This is another activity that will benefit from the perspectives of others who know you well. Consider working through it with a friend or family member to increase your awareness of how you may come across to others.

1. Reflect on what you know about yourself and your leadership style
2. Complete the phrases below
3. Meet with your staff individually or as a team for the purpose of getting to know one another

Complete these phrases:

- I think of a team as being like a _____

  _____

- I think of my role on the team as _____

  _____

- My communication style tends to be _____

  _____

- Under stress, it may be more like _____
  _____

- My approach to giving performance feedback is _____
  _____

- I appreciate feedback from others when/if it is _____
  _____

- You'll know I'm pleased when you see/hear me _____
  _____

- You'll know I'm displeased when you see/hear me _____
  _____

- During my military transition, I may need your help learning to _____
  _____

- To build strong relationships with me and the team, please
  avoid doing/saying _____
  _____

- As a manager, my pet peeves are _____
  _____

By completing this activity, you will enhance your leadership
skills in a civilian context. The insight gained from reflecting and
responding to the questions will further solidify your integration
and effectiveness as a leader in your new environment.

Moving Forward: Action Steps for Success

Reflection for Veterans

Purpose: To capture your observations and insights about the Integrating
process, and apply them to your own transition experience

Directions: Reflect on the chapter and complete the following prompts

1. My understanding of the Integrating stage is:

_____

_____

_____

_____

_____

_____

_____

_____

2. I identify with the following aspects of the Integrating stage:

_____

_____

_____

_____

_____

_____

_____

_____

3. Based on what I've learned about myself and Integrating, I need to do or be aware of the following things in order to avoid missteps:

_____

_____

_____

_____

_____

_____

_____

By engaging in this reflective process, you'll gain a deeper understanding of your personal integration journey. This self-awareness will not only help you navigate your current transition more effectively but also provide valuable insights that can guide your future career decisions and personal growth in the civilian world.

Closing Thoughts

Employers: While you can't provide definitive timelines for when new-hire service members will feel fully integrated or be considered for promotion, you can offer reassurance and support throughout their journey. Your capacity to be patient with the process and show faith in the individual will go a long way toward accelerating the transition into integration.

Creating opportunities for integrated veterans to support the transition success of military new hires is a win-win for all concerned, and it strengthens the bond between them and your organization. Don't be afraid to ask your integrated veterans for help—my experience is that they will be both happy and proud to oblige!

Veterans: Integration marks a significant milestone in your transition from military to civilian life. As you reflect on your journey, recognize the progress you've made and the unique insights you've gained. This newfound perspective isn't just about adapting to civilian life—it's about leveraging your military experience to excel in your new environment. Your integration story can serve as an inspiration and guide for others following in your footsteps. Consider how you might use your experiences to mentor fellow veterans or educate civilian colleagues about the value of military background in the workplace.

Part 3

In the Loop with Employers' Point of View

About this section:

What: Organizational recipe for success

Who: Written for employers, with insight for veterans

Why: To help organizations retain the veterans they hire

How: Through research, anecdotes, theoretical models

When the first edition of *Field Tested* was published in late 2011, there were few if any resources available to organizations seeking to employ veterans. I was already a decade into my consulting work with veterans and military transition, but the hiring market as it pertained to veterans was new to every aspect of the employment lifecycle. So I was invited to write *Field Tested* as a guide to anything and everything related to hiring, managing, and retaining veterans.

Since that time, much has been established to support employers and veterans looking to work together. A resource I developed and continue to nurture ten years later is a group on LinkedIn called the Military Transition Interest Group (https://www.linkedin.com/groups/2041002/). Today it has over 8,000 members representing veterans from every branch of service, and employers across industries and sectors. The purpose of the group was and is to connect veterans to jobs. Readers are welcome to join at no cost. The fact that the group continues to grow weekly is evidence of its sustained relevance.

Information on résumé-writing and job search is abundant and can easily be found online; therefore, they are not covered in *At Ease*. By now you know that my voice is very different from others writing about military transition. I approach it from the point of view of business management, behavioral science, and the experience of hundreds of veterans who have generously shared their stories with me over the last two decades. The following section offers insights, lessons learned, and proven best practices I have gleaned over the last twelve years helping organizations and veterans find success with one another.

Chapter 10

Recruiting for Retention

"If you're only using the new hire for what he did in his last job, you're going to miss out on a lot of capabilities and experiences that that individual has that could help the firm. Even in areas that are unanticipated. For example, I'm doing a job right now that was completely unanticipated. The second thing is for the individual. He or she is going to be frustrated by the fact that he or she has skills that aren't being used, and mostly because the organization doesn't know he or she has those skills or experiences."

—OFFICER, USAF[37]

Understanding the Landscape: What You Need to Know First

Leverage Data Before Making Decisions

A KEY METRIC ASSOCIATED WITH EFFECTIVE RECRUITMENT IS RETENTION. There is no room for growth if an organization's recruiting resources are focused on pushing a revolving door of replacement hiring. It is costly to replace employees, especially in an organization whose goal is to grow. So, smart organizations connect the dots between recruiting and retention before they leave the gate, so to speak.

Recruiting for retention is understanding the importance of a candidate's fit with organizational culture and expectations. In other words, is the person likely to perform and remain engaged over time, given the realities of how things work day to day? Effective recruiters pay some attention to fit by getting to know their organization both in terms of its mission, its business goals, and its personality if you will. This is helpful when recruiting anyone, not just a former service member. The first section of this book explained how very different the military's organizational personality is from just about any other type of organization. It stands to reason that recruiting for retention might look a little different for former service members. Consider taking the Organizational Readiness Assessment you completed in Chapter 2 to the next level by researching the following questions.

1. How have former service members done in the past regarding:
   - Cultural integration/fit?
   - Time-to-performance (time it takes them to become productive)?
   - Sustained performance?
   - Career progression?
   - Retention?

2. Do you have a track record to look back on to learn which military hires have been successful and, based on that, what to look for in potential employees? If not, consider the following best practices:
   - Ask around for anecdotal information. Line managers are a great place to start. "Say, do you remember Joe who came to

us from the Army a few years back? Why did he decide to leave?" You may need to probe for the small "whys" beneath the big "why." For example, you learn that Joe left because he got a better offer somewhere else. Why was Joe receptive to the offer? Did he find it or did it find him? You may learn that Joe was never really happy in your organization. Why was that? If his manager can't answer this question, I guarantee that that in itself is a useful piece of information. In the military, managers know and stay involved with each and every direct report. No one falls off the radar. Likewise, in successful civilian organizations, managers know and stay involved with employees and every direct report. Remember, people leave managers, not organizations.

Go to the source by surveying, interviewing, or holding focus groups with key groups:

- current employees who served in the military
- former employees who served in the military (if you are permitted to do so)

For example, you might say, "Jane, you have been a successful employee here at Company X for many years. What would you say has contributed to that? What were your initial challenges transitioning here from the Navy? What and who helped you to overcome those challenges? How? What have been your keys to success? How would you advise military new hires who want to be successful here?"

- Interview internal human resource professionals in your organization and beyond. "In general, do former military service members tend to succeed and stay here? What do you think contributes to their tendency to stay or go? What aspects of our organization's culture or personality help or hinder their success and satisfaction?"

- If your organization permits, conduct exit interviews with all departing employees to identify primary and secondary reasons for terminating, and analyze results in terms of veteran or non-veteran status.

Be a data hound and query your human resource information system (HRIS). Sample queries:

- How many past or present employees indicate veteran status?
- Of this group, what is/was their tenure? Career progression? What are their performance ratings?
- How do the answers to these questions differ compared to the larger employee population?

Regardless of the method you use to gather intelligence, the information you get as a result may lead you to form hypotheses about the type of veteran you want to look for in the recruiting process. For example, you may see that junior enlisted service members tend to succeed and stay in certain types of jobs or divisions within your organization. That is helpful information. Or you may find that former military officers don't seem to perform as well or stay as long in certain positions as their peers hired from careers in industry.

Chances are that for every hypothesis you make based on the information you gather, many more questions will be raised in the process. The extent to which your organization seeks answers to those questions is the extent to which it will differentiate itself in the market as a veteran-friendly employer of choice. But remember, a little bit of organizational intelligence is better than no organizational intelligence when it comes to recruiting for retention.

Understand the Military Résumé

Have you ever seen the résumé of someone who has spent his or her career in the military? It will likely be very different and require a different approach from screeners and recruiters. A bit of context: service members have never had to compile their professional experience in a format we know as a résumé. Nor do they have civilian experience or terminology to translate their duties in terms that would be meaningful to the civilian reader. The résumé will likely contain unfamiliar acronyms, references, and descriptions that don't readily map to open jobs you're trying to fill. Oh, and the résumé may well be four-plus pages in length.

While HR may want to blame the veteran—and individual service members do need to get smarter about developing their civilian résumés—we as managers and HR professionals need to get better at interpreting these military résumés. If we don't make the effort, we can't claim the prize of bringing on board a phenomenal new employee.

Currently there are three basic résumé formats in use: chronological, functional, and a hybrid of the two. Each has its pluses and minuses, and recruiters have their own preferences for one format or another. That being said, studies show the chronological format to be most commonly used and preferred by recruiters.

The chronological format presents a professional development trajectory over time, in which the earliest job is often the most junior, followed by roles of increasing skill and responsibility. The reader can infer, therefore, that the first job listed—the most recent job—represents the highest level of mastery and accomplishment in a candidate's career.

However (and here's the rub), a military career doesn't necessarily progress this way. For example, responsibility for a large staff may be viewed by civilian employers as a sign of strong leadership experience. But for a career service member, that large staff may have been three jobs ago, followed by roles that were smaller in scope from a staff management perspective but much greater in scope of access to people and information, influencing leaders and strategy, etc. So a civilian recruiter could potentially read this evolution in the chronological résumé as a backward step in leadership ability.

This explains why so many former military personnel become frustrated in their early civilian roles. The recruiting process focuses on the most recent job on the résumé, which prevents the organization from recognizing, hiring, and leveraging the full contribution of the service member. The conceptual shift we are called to make is to look at a military résumé through a different lens, even if—perhaps especially if—both are in chronological format. This is how we can see the full value of a military career and compare it to other candidates coming from civilian or academic careers.

Think of it this way: a civilian career often looks like a climb up from one position to another, better position; the military career can look like a trek through various positions whose importance does not necessarily proceed vertically but, rather, laterally across time.

Career Trek vs. Career Climb

Military Career Trek   Civilian Career Climb

Do you need to become fully fluent in "militarese" to hire veterans? No. Do you need to work differently to understand what veterans bring to the table? Definitely. If you don't completely understand what you're reading on a résumé, how do you figure it out? The quickest, easiest way is to enlist the help of veterans who already work in your organization. Such individuals will likely be happy to help you translate the résumé of a fellow service member. If your organization has an employee resource group (ERG) for veterans, they can make a tangible contribution by providing support with résumé translation, candidate interviewing, and new-hire mentoring programs.

Interview Candidates

The interview is how you're going to get the information you need about the military job candidate. Because you don't read "militarese" and the candidate neither translates into civilian nor has experience interviewing for jobs, your ability to ask the right questions will be key to success, for both you and the veteran. It is well worth any extra time and effort you may need to put into the interview if you get the best possible candidate for the job you're filling.

Here are a few basics to consider, courtesy of a few veterans:

"Take the time to explain to potential candidates about the hiring process. Most of the time this is the military person's first encounter with a corporate recruiter, and I think a lot of military personnel get nervous dealing with the recruiter because they don't know or understand the hiring process."

—ENLISTED SERVICE MEMBER, USMC[38]

"If you know you're hiring a former military person ... realize they had a lot of responsibility, worked under stress and pressure, and can probably offer a lot more leadership capacity than others. You have to help harness it."

—ENLISTED SERVICE MEMBER, USAF[39]

"Explain that many positions that they will consider won't be for management and they may have to start at the technical level while they hone and demonstrate their managerial skills."

—ENLISTED SERVICE MEMBER, US ARMY[40]

Below are seven secrets to success when interviewing military job candidates:

1. *Do your homework.* During the interview you will be asking the candidate to translate his or her military experience into civilian terms, so it is only fair that you, the hiring or HR manager, be prepared to explain the job opening in jargon-free terms. Also, come prepared to describe:
   a) What success looks like in the job.
   b) What success looks like in the organization.
   c) The personality of the organization as a whole (otherwise known as culture).

Use what you've learned in this book to anticipate questions the candidate may have and to offer insight and information that the candidate may not know to ask for. Finally, educate yourself as to the basics of the military rank structure so you know who to look for when you screen résumés and candidates. For example, if you want to fill an entry-level position, a candidate who left service as a noncommissioned officer (e.g., E-8) might not be the best long-term fit. This is not to discourage you from considering every promising candidate, simply to increase your odds of retention by making relative comparisons between the civilian role and previous military rank.

2. *Suspend judgments about the candidate based on his or her résumé.* See previous reference to career trek vs. career climb!

3. *Focus on capability rather than equivalent job history.* Ask about the types of tools and technology used, the types of equipment licenses and training received. When looking at the job requisition you're trying to fill, think in terms of essential job functions rather than "nice to have" degrees and certifications.

> "It is too easy for a prospective employer to say, 'He drove a tank. We don't have tanks here.' This same employer does not understand that the tank has a computer, laser, radar, whatever. It is not a tank but a highly complicated piece of equipment. Similar to a piece of lab equipment or a production line component. Line Management needs to have the ability to look ahead when interviewing a veteran: 'This vet served his country for X number of years. He has proven he is teachable and trainable. Our company needs employees that we can train and teach who will stay with us.' This is some of the value veterans bring to civilian employers."
>
> —ENLISTED SERVICE MEMBER, US NAVY[41]

> "Ask about the decisions and choices the veteran had to make … look beyond education. Many veterans have more worldly experience than they are given credit for. Figure out how to weigh and give credit for military experience and utilize the talent that's there."
>
> —ENLISTED SERVICE MEMBER, USAF[42]

> "Ask what they did, how the experiences helped them, and how they could help a company. E-4+ have some type of supervisory experience whether they realize it or not. Ask what they did to help those they supervised."
>
> —ENLISTED SERVICE MEMBER, US NAVY[43]

Further, push hiring managers to think in these terms as well, lest they pass over outstanding candidates. (The other side of this coin is that some veterans will pass you by as potential employers if they see a list of requirements they can't meet. It won't be obvious to them which are essential vs. desired.)

See the sample set of interview questions on pages 146-148, and I encourage all readers—civilian and military—to review them with care. Service members should consider their responses to the questions, as they may well come up in actual interviews.

4. *Ask for the story.* The previous section on résumés gives us a big clue about how to interview: we need to view the candidate's military career as a whole rather than culminating in the most recent position he or she held. Armed with this insight, we simply need to draw the story out of the candidate, stopping as often as needed to clarify what's not clear. Think of it as a process of mutual discovery. Ask about key skills learned and used in the different jobs, about the results that were achieved and the impact of those results on the mission. And, to get a bird's-eye view of the individual's commitment, determination, and grit, ask about the barriers they had to overcome in order to get the job done.

5. *Describe the job.* You and the candidate have mutually supportive goals: you need to fill a position and they need a job. A spirit of collaboration can be helpful in the interview process, as a way of putting you both at ease and making the most of the interview time. I suggest placing the job description beside the candidate's résumé so you can both go over it and figure it out together. Remember that you are recruiting for retention here, so don't oversell the position or the organization just to close the requisition. Our surveys of former

service members tell us that they tend to become disillusioned if the job is not how it was described during the interview process, and they will quit due to lack of fit with the organizational culture. The same could probably be said of all job candidates, but it really holds true with service members. We must establish realistic expectations of the place and the role in order to recruit for retention.

6. *Use behavioral interview questions.* Describe a scenario and ask candidates how they would respond to it. Or ask candidates to describe a scenario and how they accomplished the objective or overcame an obstacle. This lets you in on how the individual assesses and responds to situations that could arise in the course of doing the job you're trying to fill. The key here is to limit the scenarios to things that could or would occur—keep them relevant. Not sure where to start? You can always open with a word of thanks for the candidate's military service.

7. *Ask about community-building activities.* Military job candidates may not think to mention them, but you should because they speak volumes. Because military life includes work, family, and community, many things we civilians might call team-building or employee-appreciation events are standard weekend activities for service members. Planning and coordinating a cookout for five hundred or cleanup of a ten-mile stretch of shoreline is no big deal. Further, many military roles and missions involve community building at local levels. Therefore, you will learn a lot about the candidate's abilities by asking about this type of activity. It will fill out the picture of true leadership experience by illustrating how the candidate took something from concept to execution, built coalitions of support, leveraged resources, conquered interpersonal barriers, and led a team to success.

Practical Application for Employers: Transition-Focused Interview Questions

Interview Questions

Your goal is to understand the various roles, responsibilities, skills, and experience the candidate has accumulated over the course of his or her military career. To do this, you may need to look well beyond the most recent position, going back ten years. Remember, unlike a civilian résumé that often culminates in the highest level of responsibility to date, the military résumé must be viewed as a collection of experiences to be considered together as a whole.

1. General opening questions, to build rapport and sense where individuals are in their transition from military service to civilian employment: "I know leaving the military can be a big transition ..."
   - How is it going, separating from military service?
   - How has the adjustment been?
   - What has been the biggest surprise about the civilian workplace?
   - What opportunities are you looking forward to taking advantage of as a civilian employee?
   - What challenges do you foresee as a new civilian employee?

2. For each job over the past ten years, ask:
   - How would you describe this position in layman's terms?
   - What was your primary mission in this job?
   - What did it take to accomplish this mission?
   - What were the key activities you performed, and in what circumstances?

- What people or resources were you responsible for in this role?
- What were the greatest challenges in the role?
- What is an example of a time that everything went as planned?
  - o What was your contribution?
  - o What did you learn from the experience?
  - o How did you incorporate what worked and what you learned?
- What is an example of a time that things did not go as planned?
  - o What went wrong?
  - o What did you do? (What was your contribution?)
  - o What did you learn from the experience?
  - o What did you change or do differently as a result of this experience?
- What aspects of this role or job would you like to find in a civilian position?
- What aspects of this role or job would you prefer not to perform in a civilian position?

3. General questions:
   - How would you approach a situation in which _____ (describe something typical of the job being applied for)?
   - What kinds of things did you coordinate and accomplish in the community (e.g., community social events, charitable projects, leadership roles)?
   - Looking across your recent (past ten years) military work experiences, what key knowledge, skills, abilities, and experiences would you say are most valuable?

o Setting aside the specific job you were required to do, what activities do these knowledge, skills, abilities, and experiences prepare you to do?

o How do you imagine yourself applying them in a civilian setting?

Areas to be covered in addition to benefits:

- Where they should report for work on their first day, and at what time
- Manager's name and contact information
- Forms they need to turn in, when, and to whom
- What, if anything, they need to bring
- Dress code
- What they should expect in the first days and weeks of learning and trying to perform

Make the Hire

This is an important time to remember that the person you are going to hire does not have a lot of experience evaluating job offers. In the military, you go where they send you and where you're needed, and you learn to do the job at hand. In exchange for this service, the military handles all your benefits, taxes, salary adjustments, etc. Be careful not to make assumptions about the candidate's understanding of logistical details, and take extra care to ask questions and answer questions. Often, the military new hire lived and worked on a base that also held a gymnasium, dining, shopping, and other facilities in one common area. Be sure to cover the basics, even if they seem obvious to you. See the next page for things to cover in addition to benefits.

Closing Thoughts

Employers: On a related note, this will likely be the first time the service member has been in a position to negotiate for a higher salary, although many civilian recruiters bank on limiting salaries for new hires as a way of keeping costs low. However, this can trigger the hire-replace cycle when the new employee learns that his or her colleagues earn more for the same job. It may be distasteful to think of employees talking about such things, but in the military it is transparent; salary is literally an open book. If the recruiter is misleading or takes advantage of the service member's lack of civilian experience, it can easily reflect badly on the whole organization and draw a bold black line between you and attrition. The military is large, but the community of veterans is close. To avoid becoming known as a bad place to work, and to ensure you become known as a veteran-friendly employer of choice, you have to do the right thing during the hiring process by making a fair and competitive offer.

Service Members/Veterans: Beware of bad advice related to the civilian recruiting process. Specifically, many still believe they should not disclose disability status. It is your choice, of course, but know that employers are prohibited from discriminating against candidates and employees with disabilities (https://www.eeoc.gov/publications/ada-your-employment-rights-individual-disability). Further, employers want and need to understand how to help you succeed in their organizations, and they do that by understanding what if any **accommodations** you need. They won't know if you don't tell them. If you indicate no need for accommodations during the hiring process, but then request an accommodation after you've been hired, it may leave the employer feeling you were less than forthcoming in the hiring process.

Another common misconception among veterans and service members is that they will and should be hired at a level commensurate with their military grade. This idea often leads to disappointment and disillusionment in the job-seeking process, when they are offered positions deemed to be lower in rank. It is a common practice in the civilian world to hire any employee—not just veterans—at a level where they are most likely to succeed and quickly progress. This is a lower risk than hiring someone at a senior level and seeing them flounder or fail. It benefits both parties—the employer and the new hire—to position new hires for early success and upward trajectory (promotion). Your military experience, skills, wisdom, and contribution will likely come into play once the learning curve is achieved. Patience.

Finally, if you don't plan on using your GI Bill benefit, I strongly encourage you to reconsider. Use it. Go to a reputable school. When *Field Tested* came out 12+ years ago, it didn't matter so much what school you went to because employers were hot to hire veterans and didn't focus on that. But things have changed in the last decade, and while hiring veterans is still important to many hiring organizations, the job market is competitive. Iffy online degrees from unaccredited schools won't stand up to reputable institutions others have on their résumés. I'm not saying you need an Ivy League degree, because you don't. But be smart about selecting where to use your GI Bill benefit so it truly serves your personal growth and position in the job market.

Chapter 11

Onboarding: Engage Early and Often

"I think if either an individual coach or a formal class was provided to people coming out of the military saying, 'Hey, this is what our organization is all about, here's how we operate, here's how we are different from the military and things you need to be aware of' early in their tenure, it would be very helpful. It would have been huge for me; I wouldn't have floundered so much my first year or been so frustrated or tempted to leave my company."

—OFFICER, USAF[44]

Understanding the Landscape: What Is the Importance of Onboarding Veterans?

ONBOARDING IS THE PROCESS of bringing a new hire up to speed as an employee of your organization. There is no one right way to do this. Large organizations tend to have formal structures for onboarding, such as an orientation training class, while small organizations tend to be less formal and may limit onboarding to walking the new hire around to meet everyone in the office. The expectation is that all that needs to be learned will be learned on the job rather than in a classroom. This chapter focuses on:

- The connection between onboarding and retention
- Onboarding needs of veterans
- Seven great tips for onboarding veterans

I've designed veteran onboarding programs for many companies across industries. They share something in common. In the needs assessment phase of work, we talk to veterans currently employed in the organization. What we hear is so thematic across client organizations regardless of industry, so we can say with confidence that days 0–90 are key to employee engagement and retention. (Day 0 refers to the period between the job offer and the first day of work.) We advise our clients to "flood the zone" with communication, resources, and support during these earliest days, because a veteran's (and any new hire's) first impressions can set a lasting tone and be hard to overcome later.

The Connection Between Onboarding and Retention

Onboarding is important because it contributes to retention. It is, after all, the new employee's first impression of the organization with which they have found employment. *The interest and effort put into receiving the new hire is an organization's greatest opportunity to build a bond and engage the employee as a loyal member of the team, rather than just another interchangeable worker.* Employee engagement is an ongoing need to retain your talent, and it cannot be accomplished in a day. Rather, it should be embedded into the objectives of all employee programs and messaging. Employees who feel part of an organization they admire are more likely to stay than those who feel disconnected or undervalued. This is especially true for former service members who experienced "extreme" onboarding in the military in the form of boot camp or officer candidate school!

Smart companies are reframing onboarding as a series of activities and events that occur throughout an individual's first twelve months of employment. Busy people learn best when the lessons coincide with their need for information. Therefore, inundating a room full of new hires with an introduction to the company from A to Z will not yield optimal results, as the new hires can only take in so much. Providing information and training when it can be applied is a better approach.

Be deliberate about planning your onboarding strategy. If you decide not to offer a class, have a rationale for the decision and offer another way to get people up to speed quickly. If you decide to offer a more formal program like a class, ensure it is relevant and applicable rather than a "check-the-box" activity. Investing a bit of time in a discussion of what new employees need and want in order to be successful quickly pays dividends in the form of retention. Grandinetta Group is committed to seeing service members start on strong footing. To this end, we offer the Accelerated Military Transition Course to organizations of any size, in scalable formats. We can make the onboarding program easy for organizations.

Navigating the Journey: How Veterans' Onboarding Needs May Differ

Nowhere is onboarding more important than with former military service members. They need organizational context in addition to information specific to mission and vision. Remember, veterans are coming from a very strong culture in which most processes and procedures are codified and explicit. Is this how you would describe your organization? If not, chances are good you will need to spend some time making the implicit explicit, explaining things that seem obvious to you or that are obvious to new hires coming from nonmilitary organizations. While every organization's culture and operations are different, those differences are small compared to the quantum difference between military culture and civilian culture.

Your onboarding approach for veterans doesn't have to be elaborate. As I said earlier, the most important thing is that you give it some thought and advance preparation. It should scale to your business needs and objectives. *If you only hire one or two veterans a year, then think about having a one-to-one chat once a week for the first month as well as providing the new hires with resources to peruse on their own.* If you hire lots of service members or know that you are going to in the near future (e.g., because of a new client contract or organizational initiative), think about something more formally structured, like an orientation/transition class during the first day or week of employment.

Whatever the right size and structure for you may be, it is key to have the veteran in mind and feature information they aren't likely to know or even think about (e.g., that your organization has a formal structure but is flexible with the market and can shift every eighteen months or so). A few examples of how to implement tailored onboarding are:

- Develop a stand-alone onboarding program for veterans.
- Integrate content for veterans with existing new-hire orientation material.
- Compile an information packet for new hires who are veterans, to include:
  - info about the organization's purpose, structure, and clients served
  - info about the new hire's division or team, what it does, and how that supports the larger organization's goals

   ○ info about the new hire's role on the team and clients to be served

   ○ how employee performance is measured

   ○ vocabulary/language

Moving Forward: Action Steps for Success

Best Practices in Veteran Onboarding (Not Just for Veterans!)

1. *Curate the veteran's experience.* Work with your organization's ERG for military/veterans if you have one, to put care and thought into each contact with veteran new hires. Starting from Day 0 when they get their offer, and extending at least until the end of month 2, be systematic and organized in your communication, support, and programming for your veterans. A veteran's first couple of civilian jobs may be nerve-racking for them, and they will remember how the company welcomed them and stayed connected in the earliest days.

2. *Assign a learning buddy.* Match the veteran new hire with a tenured and successful veteran, with whom the new hire can connect based on the shared experience of having served in the military. There will be a natural level of trust early on, based on the shared experience, and the new hire will be able to ask questions they may not be comfortable asking others. The military are a helpful bunch, especially when it comes to helping their own; your current employees who previously served will likely jump at the chance to mentor a "newbie." This will not only accelerate learning but strengthen the bond between the new hire and your organization because it is a show of support. Military organizations typically assign a mentor to junior personnel, so this is a comfortable role for veterans to take on. Ensure that the roles of mentor and mentee are clear, with accountabilities in place to guarantee purposeful interaction and outcomes.

3. *Engage the family.* One thing that differentiates the military from the civilian way of life is the involvement of family. Because military service is a 24/7 operation and service members usually live on the base where they work, the boundaries between work life and personal life overlap. The result is a strong sense of community that includes the whole family. So to help with the transition and to engage new hires early, including a veteran's immediate family makes a real difference. If orientation activities or materials can include the partner, it will go a long way toward early engagement of the employee.

4. *Set expectations.* The previous chapter on recruitment talked about the importance of setting clear expectations during the interview process to avoid unpleasant surprises down the line. The same goes for the onboarding process. It is another key opportunity to clarify expectations and organizational norms and to prepare the service member for early success. *Remember, veterans come to you from a different world, culturally speaking, so check your assumptions at the door in terms of what they'll know about your organization's world, and make the implicit explicit.* Consider the suggestion of an enlisted USMC veteran:

"Many enlisted are used to being told when they could leave work. This isn't the case as a civilian. The civilian manager should explain the basic rules for arriving at work, when they can leave, lunch breaks, dress code, cultural norms, etc."[45]

For example, you might say something like, "I value your skill and experience in this line of work and want to ensure your success by letting you know how we think about and execute work here at Company X."

5. *Give a warm welcome.* I wish I had a dollar for every time I've heard about a new employee showing up on their first day, only to be met with a blank stare as if no one knew to expect them. The few minutes it takes

to scurry around and find out who this new person is and where they're supposed to go makes a lasting first impression—and not the good kind. This goes for any new employee, of course, but especially for the service member who may already feel like a bit of an outsider on day one. If you accept the premise that onboarding is key to retention because it builds an early bond, then you'll understand how small oversights can have big impacts. Start things off on the right foot by anticipating the veteran's first day of employment and being prepared to receive them.

6. *Check in periodically.* Because service members "don't know what they don't know" about civilian operations and culture, it often won't occur to them to ask about how to do their jobs. Rather, like most new hires, veterans learn a lot by making mistakes and potentially embarrassing faux pas. And because service members come to their civilian organizations with years of work experience, it is easy for us to assume they know how to operate effectively and that they'll ask if they don't. The issue is not usually job knowledge but understanding *how* a job gets done in your environment. Chances are the nuts and bolts of accomplishing work are different from how work is accomplished in the military, so it is crucial that a manager or internal HR professional check in with the new employee periodically to gauge how things are going, answer questions, address concerns, check assumptions, and calibrate expectations. Additionally, use these points of contact to establish a strong personal connection and build engagement.

"I was assigned work to do and left to go do it. Now, after knowing more about my actual tasks, this was fine, but for a long time I wasn't confident that I was moving ahead in the same direction as management on my tasks and dealings with other company employees."—Enlisted service member, USN[46]

7. *Connect them to a community.* If you have an Employee Resource Group or similar network for employees who serve or served in the military, connect them to veteran new hires as early in the onboarding process as possible. It provides veterans with the sense of community they may miss, encourages networking and collaboration, and, again, builds a bond to the organization. Sometimes things we're uncomfortable asking about are more easily addressed with someone who has shared our life experience. This is not unique to veterans; smart companies find that providing such forums serves other groups as well, such as women and minority groups. It doesn't have to cost much; in fact, all it takes is one person willing to organize an occasional get-together. Take care, however, not to overuse such groups to the degree that they become a point of division rather than a point of diversity, equity, and inclusion.

Closing Thoughts

Now, if you really want to hit it out of the park and stand out as a veteran-friendly employer of choice, you'll put some thought into preparing your organization to integrate service members by providing information and awareness along the way (versus just when hired). Many employees will not have worked with or have known a veteran before and may be surprised by the cultural norms they bring with them from the military. During the transition process—that is, as your organization transitions into a veteran-friendly organization—it can be useful to think about messaging and resources for nonveteran employees regarding working with veterans. Consider providing employees with some basic information about veterans, such as a "Military Basics" training module.

Chapter 12

Performance Management

"To most civilians, what they do is a job. They have another life, they have a family, they have priorities, and this is just one of the boxes of their life. Understanding that they work this in, you try to motivate them to make what they do as a job much more of a calling, or an investment that they feel committed to."

—OFFICER, US ARMY[47]

Understanding the Landscape: What Veterans Need to Know About Performance

THERE ARE A WEALTH OF BOOKS ON MANAGING EMPLOYEE PERFORMANCE, and I won't reinvent the wheel here, but I will instead focus on the aspects that are unique to veterans. As with the other topics covered in this book, you can apply much of the thinking to other employee groups as well, so that you increase overall retention. However, I'll explain how and why the concepts are especially important for your veterans. Specifically, this chapter looks at:

- The link between performance management and retention
- Explaining metrics
- Success factors and derailers
- Feedback mechanisms and approaches
- Managing and leading staff

Performance Management and Retention

As you know by now, military service members are used to executing against a mission. There is a sense of importance and an expectation of excellence (remember the stakes). Therefore, veterans will want and expect to be as successful as civilian employees of your organization. To enhance retention, it's crucial to accelerate the cultural learning curve for veterans and support their on-the-job success. If, on the other hand, the veteran is left to sink or swim, to learn every lesson the hard way—through real-time trial and error—and to feel alone in the drive for success, the organization can hold itself accountable for premature attrition.

While service members are adept at quick learning and using their wits to navigate new situations, it's important to recognize the differences between military and civilian work environments. Don't get me wrong. Service members are quick learners and accustomed to using their wits and experience to figure things out on the fly. This approach works in the military because:

- Everyone is working together toward shared goals.
- Everyone has a common understanding of roles and performance standards.
- A team of peers and leaders is fully vested in the success of the individual.

How does your organization's culture compare to these military norms? While some similarities may exist, the differences are often significant due to the distinct nature of civilian missions. Chances are, you are hitting the mark to some extent on one or more of the elements. But because your organization's mission is different from the military's mission, it probably looks a bit different. That's fine; the goal is not to change your organization's culture to sync with what the veteran is used to. The key is to set and manage the veteran's expectations early on, clarifying how and why success occurs differently in the civilian workplace. Here are some tips from the front:

> "Most veterans are self-motivated because they have a sense of duty and professionalism to perform and get the job done. Don't micromanage them. Many, especially if they ranked E-6 or above, have had experience leading and directing others. Give them the task, the authority to accomplish it, any parameters they need to work within, and let them do what they do best."
>
> —ENLISTED SERVICE MEMBER, USAF[48]

> "Challenge them. Service members are used to goals and objectives. Give them some along with certain parameters and then let them go. Reel them back in as necessary, but chances are they will deliver results you did not expect."
>
> —ENLISTED SERVICE MEMBER, US COAST GUARD[49]

Explaining Metrics

While many service members have experience managing budgets, staff, and resources, they do not have experience doing it in a context that measures performance daily on the New York Stock Exchange. For this reason, priorities are different regarding metrics, and you want to be clear about what they are in your organization.

Remember the translator tool from Chapter 3 (select a *word or concept* used by your organization, interpret the word or concept according to its *practical meaning*, further break down the word or concept into *concrete behaviors* that exemplify it, and articulate the organization's formal or stated *expectations*)? It can be very helpful in breaking down how performance is measured in your organization. Useful for all new employees: yes. Essential for former service members: absolutely. Performance metrics are thought of differently in the military, with greater emphasis placed on impact to the mission and meeting grade-level expectations versus entrepreneurialism, business development, and risk taking.

I recommend a one-to-one sit-down or group training for military new hires that clearly explains, step by step, your organization's philosophy and practice regarding:

- Defining performance (e.g., five core competencies)
- Measuring performance (e.g., five-point rating scale; 360-degree input)
- Measuring impact (e.g., what results does activity yield for the organization?)
- Assessing performance (e.g., six-month check-in in the first year followed by an annual review)
- Assigning meaning (e.g., a rating of "on track" is considered acceptable in year one, but the employee must meet the minimum standard in year two)
- Rewarding performance (e.g., a rating of "on track" in year one equates to a 3 percent raise)
- Developing capability (e.g., available training, action planning)
- Correcting performance gaps (e.g., six-month window to resolve issues)

Hopefully you are having this conversation with all new hires. Regardless, you or someone on your team needs to articulate performance expectations to new hires from the military. Their only frame of reference is what's generally referred to as a "military fitness report," which aims to track the effectiveness of a massive number of personnel in the most efficient manner possible. The military culture values giving corrective feedback verbally rather than in writing, and in real time. This is important to know for two reasons:

1. If your organization provides corrective or "developmental" feedback in writing, it will come as an unpleasant shock to the veteran and create needless anxiety.

2. If your organization's culture does not value or do a good job of providing real-time feedback, but rather saves it up for the annual review, the veteran will likely feel blindsided (as anyone might).

It isn't hard to see how one or both of these experiences could undermine a veteran's feeling of being supported and positioned to succeed. New employees expect a learning curve but need to feel successful within a reasonable period of time if they are to remain motivated. Clearly establishing the veteran's expectations around measurement of and support for performance is critical to retention.

The Root of the Issue: Success Factors and Derailers

In addition to formal performance metrics, your organization probably has a lot of unwritten wisdom about what works and what doesn't. I'm referring to the cultural aspects of performance management, the "real" way to get things done successfully. To the extent it is possible to codify some of this wisdom for the benefit of new hires, it's worth the time and effort spent *making the implicit explicit*. When organizational clients ask me to do this for them, my preferred method is to conduct focus groups with staff at different grades who are, of course, former service members. Sample questions are:

- Regarding Performance Management, what do you wish someone here had told you in your:
  - first day?
  - first week?
  - first year?
- What words of advice would you give a service member joining the company?
- What is one thing a new hire should absolutely do (success factor) and absolutely not do (derailer) in order to be successful in this organization?
- What are the biggest differences between this place and the military?
- What surprised you most, as a new employee?

Navigating the Journey: How to Communicate What's Most Important About Performance

Coaching Managers

While coaching is a powerful tool for all employees, it's particularly crucial for veterans transitioning into civilian leadership roles. Over the years I have worked with many retired general officers as they made their transition from military to civilian leadership roles. Many have told me that civilian organizations lack true leadership. Furthermore, they have complained that organizations hire them for their military leadership experience but then won't allow them to lead. Organizations, on the other hand, tell me that they invest a lot of money in retired officers and receive a very low return on that investment because their style of leadership doesn't work in a civilian setting. This disconnect often leads to burned bridges and lost opportunities as former officers struggle to assimilate into the civilian workplace.

At the heart of this issue lies a fundamental misunderstanding of the term "leadership" itself. Aligning the expectations of these respective stakeholder groups begins at the most basic level imaginable: the word "leadership." We all know the word, but are we using the same definition? No. It means different things in military and civilian worlds.

In the military, leadership is ingrained from day one, with clear protocols and expectations. The organization is designed to develop leaders, with specific boundaries and activities associated with a clear mission. In contrast, civilian leadership can take many forms, often developing organically over time. Civilian leaders may or may not receive formal training, and leadership roles are often earned on the basis of good performance over time. The lack of standardized training, philosophy, and role definition in civilian environments means leadership can manifest in numerous ways, most of which may not be recognizable as leadership to former service members.

Understanding these differences in leadership approaches is crucial. To help bridge this gap, it's important to focus on effective communication and feedback strategies. The following practical applications provide tools and examples to assist both veterans and civilian managers in navigating these challenges.

Practical Application

Feedback Conversation. This illustrates a constructive feedback dialogue between a manager and a veteran employee. It demonstrates how to address performance issues while being sensitive to the veteran's background and expectations.

Giving Performance Feedback

Manager: John, I'd like to talk with you about the report you submitted yesterday. I see the effort you put into it. However, it is still lacking some key components. Specifically, you've done a nice, thorough job analyzing the data and reporting the themes, but I don't see your interpretation of what it all means, what "story" the data is telling us. Do you know what I mean?

John: Yes, sir, I think you are saying that you want me to include my personal opinion, right?

Manager: Yes, your educated point of view. (By the way, you don't need to call me "Sir.")

John: Yes, sir. I mean, okay, I will try to stop calling you that, but habits are hard to break! [they both laugh]

John: I'm not really used to including personal opinion, since in the military the boss just needed accurate facts that he could then base his own opinion on. I don't know what I'd really have to add to that in terms of my own opinion or views.

Manager: I see what you're saying. I think we're looking for something a bit different here. One thing we value about your work in the military is familiarity with this particular topic. You bring more hands-on experience than anyone else here has, and we want to learn as much as we can from you. The team can show you how to present your opinions and views in a formal report—that's the easy part. What I want to see more of is your firsthand knowledge.

John: So, for example, the theme about process gaps—you want me to say why I think those gaps are occurring, based on my experience?

Manager: Yes. And take it a step further by offering suggestions and recommendations for how we can eliminate those gaps. I'd like you to demonstrate ownership of the problem with me by proposing solutions. See what I'm saying?

John: Definitely. Wow, this job is going to be even more fun than I had thought! Hope you don't regret inviting my opinions—you may need to rein me in!

Manager: Well, we'll worry about that if and when it happens. For now, I want to hear every hypothesis and suggestion you have to offer. That's why I hired you.

John: Understood. I'll get right on it and have a revised report to you by the end of today.

Manager: Great, I look forward to seeing it. Thanks.

Coaching Questions. To further support the transition process, we offer a set of coaching questions tailored to address common challenges faced by veterans in the civilian workplace. These questions can be used by managers or mentors to guide veterans through cultural, transitional, and interpersonal challenges.

Moving Forward: Action Steps for Success

Sample Coaching Questions

Cultural Challenge

- How would you describe your current challenge?
- What have you tried so far to address the challenge?
- How effective was that approach?

- How is it similar to situations you faced in the military?
- How is it different?
- What have you observed others doing in response to similar challenges in this environment?
- How effective were those approaches?
- What could you do to more effectively address the current challenge?
- How would you see that playing out?
- What's the next step?

Transition Process

- Now that you've been here a week, how's it going?
- What has it been like for you, leaving military service?
- What routines from military life would you like to integrate into your civilian life?
- Is there anything I can do to help make that happen?
- What has surprised you the most about leaving military service?
- How are you coping with it?
- Would you be interested in helpful resources?

Interpersonal Challenge

- How would you describe the current situation?
- Can you give me a for-instance?
- What feedback have you received about it?
- How does the feedback about your impact align with your intended impact?
- Putting yourself in _____'s shoes, how could that have come across?
- What have you noticed about the organization [or team, or people] that can explain the gap?

- What approaches have you observed others using effectively in this environment?
- Why do you suppose that would be important?
- What would you be willing to do differently to achieve a better result?
- Is there anyone you'd feel comfortable checking in with to get some real-time feedback?

Practical Application

To further illustrate these concepts and provide practical guidance, let's examine a coaching conversation scenario that addresses interpersonal style challenges often faced by military new hires.

Performance Coaching on Interpersonal Style

In this scenario, military new hire Chris sits down with his Human Resources manager to express frustration with peer feedback.

HR Manager (HRM): Thanks for coming in, Chris. I'm glad you wanted to talk about what's happening on the team. I don't know a lot about it and look forward to hearing your perspective. How would you describe the current situation?

Chris: Well, to be honest with you, I don't really understand it myself. It seems like everything I do and say is wrong, and everyone feels the need to tell me about it. It's getting old.

HRM: Can you give me a for-instance?

Chris: Perfect example: yesterday we're in a peer work session discussing how to approach a problem for a client. It was two hours of going around and around, getting nowhere. I knew exactly what we should do because I've done it a hundred times in the military, but no one wanted to hear it—they just waited until I finished, then continued as if I hadn't said anything! I expected more professionalism out here in the civilian world. Yesterday was the last straw; I went back to my desk and called an Army buddy who's working over at _____ Company and loving it.

HRM: I hear your frustration. What feedback have you received about it from others?

Chris: Oh—get this—as I'm leaving the meeting, my counterpart from another team says in passing, "You're going to have to learn to play better with others if you want them to listen to you." What does that mean? I didn't come here to play, I came here to get a job done.

HRM: Anything else?

Chris: No, I never have these issues with my staff. They love me.

HRM: I'd like to be able to visualize the scenario—can you recall exactly what you said in the meeting that seemed to go unnoticed?

Chris: Sure, I said exactly what I always say, "You guys are going about this all wrong. When I was in the military we dealt with this type of breakdown all the time. Here's what we need to do …" Then I told them what we need to do. Easy.

HRM: How does the *feedback* about your impact align with your *intended* impact?

Chris: It doesn't. They don't get it. I am being as clear as I know how to be, I have the solution they say they want and we could have been done with this issue last week if they just listened. I don't see the point of all these meetings to discuss a problem that has an obvious solution.

HRM: I can see that you are communicating clearly—it just doesn't seem to be effective. What do you make of that?

Chris: I have no idea. Everyone says, "We value honesty and integrity here," but they don't seem to be able to handle a direct conversation. One time recently, two people who agreed with me in the meeting later sent me emails backpedaling, suggesting a different approach.

HRM: That is its own kind of feedback. What connection do you see between the various feedback you've received over the last few months since you started working here?

Chris: Obviously I'm doing something wrong, but can't figure out what it is.

HRM: Putting yourself in the shoes of these colleagues, how could your communication have come across? Think about it for a second. [Pause]

Chris: Maybe too direct.

HRM: What have you noticed about the organization that can explain the gap between your intention and the end result?

Chris: I've noticed that people are very polite and formal here, even at the expense of efficiency. Seems like a lack of honesty to me, like they care more about being liked than about getting the job done.

HRM: What approaches have you observed others using effectively in this environment?

Chris: I'm always impressed by Joe. Everyone likes him and he still gets results. I don't know how he does it.

HRM: It's really helpful to have someone like Joe to observe. Try to put your finger on it—what do you see him doing that might shed some light on his effectiveness?

[Pause]

Chris: He asks a lot of questions. And he's very nice to people even when they make off-the-wall comments. I don't know if I'd have the patience for that.

HRM: Why do you suppose asking questions and being patient with off-the-wall comments would be important?

Chris: It seems to get people talking and moving forward. But a lot slower than just telling them what to do.

HRM: I wonder why a peer group would respond so differently to you than your direct reports. What do you make of that?

Chris: I guess my peers don't want to be told what to do. And, given that I'm sitting here with you now says something. What should I do? I don't want to dumb myself down just to play nice.

HRM: Well, you have a clear example of another approach that seems to work: Joe's approach. What would you be willing to do differently to achieve a better result?

Chris: I guess I could try asking more questions—and not shutting people down when they make strange comments. I'd be willing to try it and see how it goes, I guess.

HRM: That sounds like a good start. Try to notice if people respond to you differently as a result. Will you let me know how it goes?

Chris: Sure. I have another peer work session next week—I'll try it out and call you afterwards.

HRM: Is there anyone in the group who you'd feel comfortable checking in with after the meeting to get some real-time feedback?

Chris: I think I could ask Joe. He's the only one who actually acknowledges my comments anyway!

HRM: Sounds like a plan. Oh—by the way—if you like the results you get, you might consider using the same approach with your direct reports. You may be surprised by their creative problem-solving skills!

This scenario demonstrates how effective coaching can help veterans navigate the nuances of civilian workplace communication and leadership styles. By fostering self-reflection and encouraging adaptive strategies, both veterans and their civilian colleagues can work toward a more harmonious and productive work environment. Does it take a bit longer than just telling them what to do? Yes, but as the previous coaching conversation illustrates, when the idea comes from the person with the issue, they have skin in the game and are more likely to retain the learning.

Closing Thoughts

As veterans transition into civilian leadership roles, it's crucial to recognize and adapt to the differences in leadership culture. Civilian organizations, driven by competitive market forces, require flexible and agile methods. This adaptability is a strength in the business landscape.

Veterans should approach these differences with an open mind and a willingness to learn, expanding their leadership toolkit. Employers can ease this transition by providing clear expectations, open communication, and supportive coaching.

Fostering mutual understanding and leveraging veterans' unique strengths can create a powerful synergy between military experience and civilian innovation, benefiting both the individual and the organization.

Chapter 13

Career Ownership & Development

"In the civilian organization I encountered something for the first time I'd never encountered in the military. And that was that there were a number of people, a fairly large number of people, who were there for a job and not a career."

—Officer, USMC[50]

Understanding the Landscape: What Is Important to Consider About Veterans and Career Development?

WHERE THE PREVIOUS TOPIC, performance management, focused on accelerating performance and articulating performance metrics, we now shift the focus to a new challenge for veterans: taking charge of their own careers.

In the military, career progression was highly structured and predictable. The hierarchy was completely transparent: no level jumping and a clear path of promotion with articulated expectations related to rate of progression. The system ran the process, and the service member was part of that process. It was highly routinized to accommodate the huge size of the organization and, in some ways, could be called paternalistic in that an individual's career path was taken care of by the system.

Now, as veterans enter the civilian workforce, they face a new paradigm. The service member is in a position to shape and drive his or her own career. This is an exhilarating adventure for many, but most veterans will, at some point, find it a bit mysterious.

Navigating the Journey: How Career Development and Retention of Veterans Are Connected

Understanding this shift from a structured military career path to a civilian career path is crucial for organizations aiming to retain veteran talent. The most common mistake I see civilian organizations make is allowing these valuable hires to walk away too easily. Let me explain what I mean. An organization that wants to retain great talent takes the long view, recognizing that some hires may not be a good fit in their jobs. If, on the other hand, they are a good fit for the organization in general, you'll want to retain them.

To effectively retain veterans, two key strategies are essential:
1. Setting realistic expectations
2. Ensuring veterans understand internal career options

If you assume that some percentage of valued new hires will leave their jobs within one to thirty-six months, wouldn't you rather move them internally than lose them altogether?

Communicating organizational commitment is crucial. The most important message you can give to military new hires is, "We value you and we want you to stay with us for a long time. As part of this corporate commitment to you as a valued member of the organization, we want you to know that there are lots of ways to be successful and happy here, so look here first before considering leaving."

This approach acknowledges a fundamental change for veterans. While serving in the military, walking off the job was not an option; it was considered a crime. Now, for the first time in their careers, former service members can exercise their right to choose. Recognize this as a possibility (as you should for all employees) and reduce risk by being transparent about career options across your organization.

Maintaining ongoing contact is another key retention strategy. Often, an individual or group of internal Human Resources professionals serve as a point of continuity for the veteran. Oftentimes line managers also play this role. Invest in the relationship with veterans by maintaining connections over time. A common complaint I hear from former service members is, "You can sink or swim out there, nobody cares. No one tells you how to be successful."

Chances are good that veterans will have career options in your organization they never had in the military. The most obvious example that comes to mind is the option to enjoy a successful career in-grade rather than seeking promotion. Every organization is different, but generally an organization needs a stable base of "solid citizen" performers who get the job done well and keep the bus on the road, so to speak.

This points to another cultural difference between the military and some civilian organizations: The military organization is dependent upon a constant cycle of promotion. The emphasis is on preparing each person for their next job, which will become available when the person currently in that job moves up to *their* next job. In the words of one officer in the U.S. Army, "In the military, when your boss asks you what your next job is, the appropriate response is, '*Your* job, boss.' Can you imagine saying that to a civilian boss?!"[51]

The military can be said to use an "up or out" model of career development, in which one is expected to progress at a prescribed rate. If one does not, one leaves the organization. The option of remaining at a junior rank simply does not exist as it does in many civilian organizations. Many of the veterans I have had the pleasure to work with over the years were delighted by the prospect of working a job they enjoy and do well, on a regular schedule, without the mandate to climb a career ladder. Especially after a career of twenty or more years in the military, many want to replace the 24/7 lifestyle with a balance of work and personal activities.

Understanding the military perspective gives you valuable insight into veterans' needs. For veterans, managing their own careers will be a big learning curve with a lot appearing to be at stake (i.e., their civilian career). The military community is well-networked and very generous about sharing leads and information. But when it comes to giving career advice, it may well be "the blind leading the blind." Why leave retention to chance; you can make a bottom-line difference by anticipating, informing, and staying connected to the veterans you hire.

Moving Forward: Action Steps for Success

As with so many other topics we've covered in this book, organizational culture plays a role in career management. It's called politics, the written and unwritten rules of the road, insiders' knowledge. You should assume insider knowledge will be unknown to the military new hire. Even after some period of tenure, if an individual hasn't given or received a promotion, chances are he or she doesn't know the nuances that go into such a decision. For example, some organizations want employees to be up-front about their career goals. Other organizations want to know their employees are ambitious, but they don't want to hear about it. Every culture is different, and we've already looked at some of the differences found in the military's transparent approach to career progression.

> "There's an expectation in the military that you're going to get promoted, that you want to advance. We don't let people stagnate. But on the civilian side, you have a lot of people who are very happy being individual contributors. They're happy being whatever level they are, and that's where they want to stay. They're not going to go out of their way to get more training or to do something more, because they don't have any desire to advance, and so understanding what motivates people in that sector is different from the true military."
>
> —OFFICER, US ARMY[52]

Practical Application: Reengaging the Disengaged Veteran

We've spent the previous pages talking about the aspects of the employee lifecycle as they pertain to engagement, performance, and retention. I'd like to turn your attention now to the important topic of reengaging veterans. In my experience, disengagement during the first three months of employment is common, especially in organizations that lack effective onboarding. I consider this period I've referred to as Day 0–90 as critical to success for all concerned. As a consultant, I am privy to insight that you the employer may not be, because my role is often to gauge employee sentiment, identify root causes, and solve for them. Below are mini-case studies that illustrate how easily veteran new hires (and other new hires) can disengage and be reengaged. My aim in sharing them is to illuminate potential organizational blind spots that contribute to attrition.

Each phase of the employee lifecycle presents challenges and opportunities for addressing—and hopefully preventing—disengagement.

- *Recruitment.* Due to a **misunderstanding in the hiring process**, Steve assumed the full cost of his relocation would be paid for by his new employer. Imagine his dismay and disillusionment when part of the expense was denied. This left a bitter taste in his mouth for some time, causing him to wonder if he had been the victim of a bait and switch. As his first few months went by, *Steve became reengaged* as a fan of the organization when it sponsored him in a technical certification course.

- *Onboarding.* Jean was left standing awkwardly in the lobby on her first day of employment, feeling like she'd shown up at a party she hadn't been invited to. Why? Nobody seemed to be expecting her or know where to send her. **Disorganized administrative processes** continued to plague her first week of employment, leading her to wonder what she'd signed up for. These thoughts were quickly forgotten, however, during the top-shelf orientation training class Jean attended the following week. All she learned about the organization and the positive connections she made with fellow new hires during the program *erased any doubt* she may have had about her decision based on first impressions.

- *Performance management.* Ideally, employee performance reviews should hold no unpleasant surprises. Unfortunately, in the real world they often do. Dale was shocked by feedback he received after what he considered a great first year with the firm. Regardless of whether it was his manager's conflict avoidance or his own defensive reaction to criticism, Dale did not expect to hear that he had missed the mark on work quality. He always met his deadlines, but, as he learned, sometimes at the expense of the end product. In the course of the performance review, Dale and his manager both realized they had made assumptions about priorities and **failed to communicate** sufficiently throughout the year. With some frustration, they got on the same page and agreed to move forward in a positive direction. A year later, this was *nothing more than a "war story"* for Dale as he received a promotion for outstanding performance.

- *Career management.* Lorraine was discouraged after being passed over for promotion two years in a row. She understood why, but it still hurt her pride and led her to wonder where her career was going. However, because she (1) felt a **strong bond** with her organization and colleagues, (2) was **committed to the work**, and (3) otherwise **felt valued** and appreciated for her effort, Lorraine had a high level of engagement in spite of her disappointment. Because of her consistently positive experiences as an employee, *she did not initiate leaving for another company* after being passed over, as someone less engaged might have done.

You may have noticed that I implied but did not specify veteran status in the examples. This was purposeful, to make a broader point. While *At Ease* focuses on the success of veterans in the civilian workplace, many of the dynamics, insights, and solutions apply to all new hires.

Closing Thoughts

In this chapter, we've explored the complexities of career management and retention for veterans transitioning into civilian roles. The shift from a structured military career progression to a more self-driven civilian approach presents unique challenges and opportunities. Veterans may find themselves navigating unfamiliar terrain, and organizations must adapt their strategies to support this transition effectively.

By aligning your organizational practices with these insights, you can better support veterans in managing their careers and ensure a smoother transition and realize ROI in the form of high engagement, performance, and retention. Applying what you've learned in *At Ease* across the board with all new hires can exponentially enhance organizational ROI, and make your organization a truly great place to work.

Conclusion

Veterans and service members, your military transition is a significant life event that includes so much more than your résumé. It is a hero's journey indeed. I want to close with a message of hope for anyone who is, understandably, feeling overwhelmed, discouraged, fearful, or uncertain. At the other end of this experience you will have a Transition Story. It will be highly inspirational and helpful to others. It will include highs and it will include lows, the challenges you overcame and the victories you achieved. You can't see it yet because YOU ARE LIVING THE STORY RIGHT NOW. When you experience a low, remember this: it is the lows and how you overcome them that will make your story helpful and inspiring.

I can't wait to hear your Transition Story! My hope for you is that the military transition experience is made easier for you by reading this book. It's why it's been named as it is: "At Ease" is not just a military reference but an affirmation from me to you.

It is my sincere hope that every reader of *At Ease* has learned about themselves through reflection, and about others through the perspectives described herein. Many of the principles apply beyond the scope of military transition, to any major life transition. In this way, *At Ease* can be a helpful resource beyond the military transition.

Employers, I hope you feel a renewed energy and commitment to your programs for veterans and all new hires as a result of reading *At Ease*. To work with me and my team at Grandinetta Group, see the Resource page that follows.

Resources

Working with Grandinetta Group, LLC

Veterans and Service Members

All services below are easily accessed at https://military.grandinetta.com/

➢ Accelerated Military Transition Course: First of its kind, a highly interactive and personalized program designed to significantly reduce the cultural learning curve you will encounter in the civilian workforce. You'll get robust online content, small-group coaching, membership in an alumni community, and all the information and insight needed to pursue a smooth and successful military transition. Most of all, you'll learn about yourself and begin to find purpose and meaning outside the military.

➢ Military Transition Framework Assessment: Free online assessment of where you are in the Military Transition Framework™, insight to what it means, and recommended next steps to help you progress, starting now!

➢ Transition Coaching: Individual and group coaching with the military transition-trained coaches of Grandinetta Group. We improve lives every day, why not yours?

Organizations/Employers Contact us directly at info@grandinetta.com or 833-923-5623

➢ Accelerated Military Transition Course (volume purchase): Our best-in-class program is available in-house to your employees. Grandinetta Group is highly collaborative, delivering as-is or customized to your organization. We make you the hero. Let's explore the possibilities!

➢ *At Ease* (volume purchase): The must-have resource for all your military hires and employee resource group members. By providing *At Ease* to your employees, you do a real service to those who have served and continue to serve our nation.

➢ Individual & Group Coaching: Grandinetta Group coaches are field tested and proven to accelerate learning and success for veterans. We also coach and train HR and line managers to ease the transition of military new hires and avoid common pitfalls and missteps. Let's talk.

➢ Consulting & Customization: Grandinetta has designed and implemented programs for some of the biggest employers in the US. We've led the industry with training for recruiting and onboarding teams, line managers, Human Resource leaders, and employee resource groups, and current/former military, of course! Contact us to discuss your needs.

➤ Booking Emily King for Speaking Engagements: Emily has been invited to share her unique and inspiring perspective for organizations including the New York Stock Exchange, Blackstone, Sodexo, and more, as well as for countless industry conferences. Contact us for pricing and availability.

Recommended Resources by Topic

Transition

- o The Accelerated Military Transition Course, by Grandinetta Group
- o *Making Sense of Life's Changes,* by William Bridges
- o *Designing Your Life,* by Bill Burnett and Dave Evans

Leadership

- o The Next Level Podcast, at https://teamperformanceinstitute.com/media/

Identity & Transformation

- o *Deep Change,* by Robert Quinn

Growth Mindset

- o *Mindset,* by Carol S. Dweck

Success

- o *The Next Level,* by Scott Eblin

○ *What Got You Here Won't Get You There,* by Marshall Goldsmith

○ *Mastery,* by George Leonard

Inspiration

○ *Finding Waypoints: A Warrior's Journey Toward Peace and Purpose,* by Terese Schlachter and Colonel Gregory Gadson (Ret.)

End Notes

1. Master Sergeant (E-7).
2. William Bridges, *Transitions: Making Sense of Life's Changes*, 40th anniversary edition (Da Capo, 2019).
3. Robert E. Quinn, *Deep Change: Discovering the Leader Within* (Wiley, 2010), 59, 66.
4. Quinn, *Deep Change*, 45.
5. Carol Dweck, *Mindset: The New Psychology of Success* (Ballantine, 2007), as summarized by Vandermont, https://www.vandermont.org/post/2-growth-mindset-what-is-it-and-how-does-it-apply-to-what-we-do
6. Carol Dweck, *Mindset: Changing the Way You Think to Fulfill Your Potential* (2017), Chapter 1.
7. Master Sergeant (E-8).
8. Navy Chief Petty Officer (E-5).
9. Captain (ret).
10. Emily King, "Military to Civilian Onboarding," ASTD *InfoLine*, Vol. 27, Issue 1013 (2010).
11. Chief Petty Officer (E-7).
12. Sergeant First Class (E-7).
13. Lt. Col. (ret).
14. Captain (ret).
15. Lt. Col. (ret).

16. Technical Sergeant (E-6).
17. Lt. Col. (ret).
18. Chief Petty Officer (E-7).
19. Master Sergeant (E-8).
20. Sergeant (E-5).
21. Lt. Col. (ret).
22. Petty Officer (E-5).
23. Petty Officer (E-5).
24. Master Sergeant (E-7).
25. Col. (ret).
26. Col. (ret).
27. Lt. Col. (ret).
28. Lt. Col. (ret).
29. Col. (ret).
30. From "Your Military Transition" audio program, by Emily King, 2009.
31. Master Sergeant (E-8).
32. Petty Officer (E-4).
33. Petty Officer (E-5).
34. Col. (ret).
35. Lt. Col. (ret).
36. Ryan Pendell, "7 Gallup Workplace Insights: What We Learned in 2020," Gallup, December 11, 2020, https://www.gallup.com/workplace/327518/gallup-workplace-insights-learned-2020.aspx
37. Lt. Col. (ret).
38. Master Sergeant (E-8).
39. Master Sergeant (E-7).
40. Chief Warrant Officer (CW-4).
41. Petty Officer (E-4).
42. Master Sergeant (E-7).
43 Senior Chief Petty Officer (E-8).
44. Lt. Col. (ret).
45. Staff Sergeant (E-6).
46. Petty Officer (E-5).
47. Col. (ret).
48. Master Sergeant (E-7).
49. Chief Petty Officer (E-9).
50. Lt. Col. (ret).
51. Lt. Col. (ret).
52. Col. (ret).

Acknowledgments

THE CHALLENGE OF MILITARY TRANSITION and the importance of the topic to service members and to private sector organizations has been a professional focus since the late '90s, when I first began to explore it. Helping others to overcome the challenge and pay attention to the topic has become a mission that feels very personal. Several people have witnessed my journey over the years and supported me with enthusiasm, sure that a day would come when a larger audience would be just as aware of it and concerned with finding solutions. Chief among these supporters have always been my family and friends, always cheering me on long before "military transition" was a thing. While "thank you" seems a woefully inadequate acknowledgment, I'll say it anyway. Thank you.

At Ease would not have happened without the enthusiastic support of the following people, to whom I express my heartfelt thanks: Jon Sanchez and the family at Team Performance Institute, Frank Ball, Brad Wenstrup, Scott Eblin, Greg Gadson, Lois Dicky of Grandinetta

Group, Peter Jensen of Team Performance Institute, Brian McNulty at Bigger Boat Studios, Jacki Seley and Jan Bayer at Written LLC, Marcella Bayer at Capacity Group, Paul Kniaz, and Michael Pett.

My heartfelt thanks go to the many men and women who generously shared their firsthand experiences, giving me a window into the personal nature of military transition. Six individuals in particular have been with me since Day One, allowing me to interview them and use their comments in various formats over the years, and who have been an informal group of advisors whose wisdom I have called upon for ongoing calibration of my ideas and understanding: Frank Ball, Jane Maliszewski, Bill Dean, Seb DeLiso, Derek Harris, and Karen Jeffries. Specific to this book, many former service members participated in interviews, surveys, and focus groups, fully throwing themselves into the effort to help their fellow service members going through the process of military transition. Many, many more have offered insight through the LinkedIn Military Transition Interest Group, and I thank them as well.

Finally, my heartfelt thanks to the many unnamed here whom I have had the privilege of coaching through their transition and who honored me with their stories, experiences, and struggles.

About the Author

Emily King is a business leader, behavioral scientist, and Master Certified Coach nationally recognized expert on the topic of the transition from military service to civilian employment. Known for her thought leadership in this space, she has been an invited speaker at the New York Stock Exchange, Blackstone, and countless national conferences. She is an award-winning author and innovator of learning and development solutions for organizations.

Emily has received formal acknowledgment for her contribution to veteran employment from former President Barack Obama, Senator John McCain, and retired US Army Generals Lloyd Austin, Raymond Odierno, and John Campbell. Emily designed and implemented the first-ever veteran transition programs at Booz Allen Hamilton and Accenture. She is the author of the award-winning book *Field Tested: Recruiting, Managing, & Retaining Veterans* (AMACOM 2012), used by Fortune 500 companies such as Comcast, Dell, Merck, Sodexo, and many others.

Field Tested received the Axiom Books Silver Medal for Business Commentary. Forging the national dialogue about veteran employment in the early 2000s won Emily the prized Wings of Change award from the Multicultural Forum on Workplace Diversity, Equity, and Inclusion.

Today Emily is president of Grandinetta Group, a leadership development consultancy whose mission statement reads, "Elevating all people and ending needless suffering in the workplace."

www.ingramcontent.com/pod-product-compliance
Lightning Source LLC
Chambersburg PA
CBHW051149120626
46547CB00012B/1001